SECRET ABOUT INFANT BAPTISM THAT EVERYONE'S MISSING

JUDY MCKENZIE MCCLARY

A STRANG COMPANY

The Secret About Infant Baptism That Everyone's Missing by Judy McKenzie McClary
Published by Creation House
A Strang Company
600 Rinehart Road
Lake Mary, Florida 32746
www.creationhouse.com

Design Director: Bill Johnson
Cover design by Terry Clifton

Library of Congress Control Number: 2007924894
International Standard Book Number: 978-1-59979-170-8

08 09 10 11 12—987654321
Printed in the United States of America

This book is lovingly dedicated to my husband, Charles, who has consistently given me support and encouragement as I researched and wrote on the essential issue of baptism and the Church.

CONTENTS

ACKNOWLEDGMENTS

THANKS TO MY FAMILY for enduring years of research and dinner table discussions, to my husband, Charles, for supporting me and walking by my side as I handed seven letters to the pastor and council members of our Lutheran church; also to our children, John Charles, Stacey Renoir, and Katesy, who have been there cheering me on during these years of research; and a special acknowledgment of our grandchildren, Lauren and Jack, for making me smile. To Jackie, my friend and sister, thank you for your cheerfulness and many means of encouragement.

Thanks to all who have prayed for this book as it was being completed, and to Creation House for their patience in readying it for publication. To the seven-member prayer group the Lord brought together to pray for me as I researched and wrote, I owe you a special debt of gratitude that only God can repay: Diane, Arlene, Sharon, Dodie, Mary Lynn, Donna, and Alice. To Delores, Sandee, and Amy, thanks for editing help.

Most of all, I thank God for entrusting me with this task.

FOREWORD

God is moving mysteriously in these last days regarding the subject of water baptism. Never before has He been so determined to bring truth to the forefront. The worldwide Church has two branches, two modes of water baptism, and teaches two wildly different ways of getting to heaven—with one branch believing that baptism saves and the other believing it does not.

This confusion can be seen in a book on the subject written by a recently retired, well-known Lutheran pastor. His book attributes the many spiritual benefits of water baptism to infant baptism. He closes his book by saying that, although a baptism of infants "can't be proved or disproved"* (it is not found in the Bible), he believes in it anyway.** Strange but true.

Another strange but true story happened recently at the same church where he was pastor. The current pastor stood before his congregation Sunday morning and related the following incident. He said the Lord told him to read the book of Ezekiel. He proceeded to obey, although he did not know the reason he was to do this. When he opened his Bible to the book of Ezekiel, however, it started to shake so hard that he quickly closed it.

He said he was on a plane flying somewhere a short time

---

* Morris Vaagenes, *Baptism God's Activity of Grace* (Minneapolis, MN: Kirk House Publishes, 2006.), 111.

** Ibid., 110.

later when he decided to try again to read the Book of Ezekiel. This time when he opened to Ezekiel, not only did his Bible shake, but so did the plane and everything in it. The pilot's frightened voice came over the intercom saying he did not know why the plane was shaking; he said everything pointed to good flying conditions. Remembering what had happened before, the pastor said he quickly shut his Bible and everything stopped shaking.

As he stood before his congregation that morning he said he was telling the story so that he could ask for thirty people to volunteer to fast for him while he tried again to read the Book of Ezekiel. That he had been asked to read Ezekiel seemed mysterious to him at the time, however, it was not at all mysterious to me. By asking the pastor to read the book of Ezekiel, I believe God was trying to get his attention so He could deliver a warning through him to the mainline denominational churches that practice an infant baptism.

My husband and I had been members of that same congregation a few years back, when God also told me to read the Book of Ezekiel. At that time, I discovered that it was in the Book of Ezekiel where the story is told of God removing His presence from the Israelite nation because of their idolatry in worshiping the goddess religions of the surrounding pagan nations.

I believe the first warning went out in the nineties to that same church in the form of the seven letters I researched and wrote, which exposed the goddess religions' connection with infant baptism. At that time the warning was ignored, even though the accuracy of the research I had done was confirmed in a front-page article in our morning newspaper within weeks after the last letter was received by that church.

The article in the *Minneapolis Star Tribune* reported a ReImagining Conference, which was held at the Minneapolis Convention Center on November 4, 1993.* At this conference, reverence and prayer was given not to Jesus Christ, as one might expect at a conference sponsored by Christian churches, but to the mystery religions' goddess named Sophia.

The conference was underwritten by a $65,000 grant from the Presbyterian Church (USA) and sponsored by the St. Paul Area Council of Churches, the Greater Minneapolis Council of Churches, and the Minnesota Council of Churches. The Evangelical Lutheran Church of America (ELCA) sent 313 people, including at least twenty staff from headquarters, while the Methodist Church sent personnel and declared the conference to be part of their women's spiritual renewal in the future.

Scripture says a good tree cannot bear bad fruit and a bad tree cannot bear good fruit. At that time, I wondered if these churches' connection to infant baptism might be the culprit, so I began to research early Church history to find out why Martin Luther had chosen to put "baptism saves" into our church's doctrinal statement rather than the statement he is so famous for—that of salvation by faith alone. I was to find conflicting interests involved in his decision and a return to an ancient heresy that the apostle Paul had warned would enter the Church after his death.

There are some who will question the right of a layperson to address the salvation practices of large and important

* Kevin Horragan, "The Afterlife: Limbo Rocked," Knight-Ridder News Service, January 10, 2006.

denominations. While it is true that I am neither a nun nor a priest, I have to ask the more educated clergy of these denominations the inevitable question, Why hasn't the controversy over infant baptism been made public from the pulpit? Why was it left for a little-known (but very curious) layperson to find out and make public?

My best guess is that you didn't know either, clergy and laypeople have been duped. *We need to join hands, repent, and get back on track.*

PART 1

DOES BAPTISM SAVE?

1

TOO MANY BAPTISMS

When I was growing up as a little girl in a Presbyterian church, I was very much aware that not all churches believed alike. My cousin, Mary, was Roman Catholic, but I would never have asked her straight out why her church taught about purgatory when ours did not.

There was another church nearby that the family of one of my sister's friends attended. Without it ever being openly discussed, I knew that church had less status than our Presbyterian church, but even though I sensed some churches were more socially accepted than others, I did not understand why.

Another thing that was never discussed in polite circles was the fact that some churches had a different baptism than ours. Again, I did not know why. As I got older and my interest in theological matters grew, I found this difference was contrary to the Bible's claim that there is only one baptism.*

I marveled at this. How could the Church so openly practice two different baptisms when the Bible says there is only one? Yet both branches seemed to believe so strongly that their baptism was the correct one. I wondered why they were

* Ephesians 4:4–6

not more concerned about the lack of unity this brought to the body of Christ. For if one examines the doctrines of various denominations as I have had the opportunity to do, water baptism is the main issue that separates them.

I also wondered why the two branches teach two such very different ways of getting to heaven. Why didn't the churches just get together and study Scripture as a team, as a unit, as friends and associates? That way, when they found out which baptism was the right one, they could all practice the same mode and attach the same meaning. Then the whole Church could be in unity.

When I began my search for the truth about water baptism, I had been a member of an infant baptism church for more than forty years. I officially joined (or I should say, my parents joined me) to the Presbyterian Church when I was just six weeks old. I don't remember it, of course, but my mother assured me it was so. Despite being over eighty, she clearly remembered that day, because when I was born she and my father could not agree on a name for me. So, it was not until the day of my baptism that I received my official name.

Usually in a Presbyterian church, the ritual of infant baptism would be conducted during a church service. However, because my parents already had four other lively little ones, it was mutually agreed to celebrate my baptism at home. The next Sunday afternoon, the Presbyterian minister and his wife came out to the farm for a fried chicken dinner and to perform the baptismal ceremony. My Uncle Jim and Aunt Sadie were invited, too. They were to "stand in" for me. Mother explained this was because I was too young to have faith for my own salvation, so they became my godparents.

With dinner finished and the dishes done, my mother took me into the back bedroom to put me into my baptismal finery. She was just finishing when my father came in. He wanted to see if we were ready and to tell her that she could name me Judy if she wished. (He had wanted to name me Sally.) Together they brought me out where the guests were and announced my name would be Judith Ann.

The three of us stood before the minister as he took out the book of rituals he carried with him for just such occasions. He opened to an infant baptism ritual and read it out loud. Then, dipping his finger into a little bowl of water, he sprinkled water on my head, no doubt adding the requisite words, "In the name of the Father and the Son and the Holy Spirit."

Another job well done! The minister probably shook hands with my parents, said good-by to the guests, chucked me under the chin, and left for home rejoicing that he had added one more soul to the great and glorious Church above and to the small Presbyterian church downtown.

Years later I wondered, Can baptism really do all the things that parents expect for infants on the day they are baptized in water? Would I indeed have gone to heaven if I had died that night? What if I had remained unsprinkled? Would God still have taken me to heaven if I had not been baptized? And where in the Bible does it say that my baptism did all that for me?

Water baptism is an interesting subject. Wars have been fought over the mode and meaning behind it. Men have been burned at the stake or drowned in a raging river because they did not agree with the official method of water baptism practiced by the state Church of their day. Women have been put in stocks and flogged because they taught other women that there was something about water baptism as taught in their church that did not quite line up with their reading of Scripture.

Anne Hutchinson, of colonial Salem, Massachusetts, was one of these believed to be full of devils because she questioned the way the Church of England and the Puritan Church of her day taught water baptism. Though she was pregnant, she was mercilessly forced to flee with her husband and children to keep from being arrested and imprisoned for her beliefs. Miscarrying because of the tragedy, it was spread about by her midwife that her undeveloped fetus was misshapen because he was the devil's offspring.*

Even earlier, in 1565, the Spanish Inquisition was already reaching itchy fingers into the southern part of what is now the United States. Its intent was to discipline residents in St. Augustine, Florida, who would not practice Church doctrine the way the official state Church of Europe wanted it practiced in the new colony. Two hundred fifty-three men, women, and infants lay dead before the ten ships sent from the mother country finished their task, raised anchor, and sailed for home.**

There are not many books written on the subject of water baptism. In daring to examine the subject, I am aware that discussing religion—and water baptism in particular—is a no-no in today's world of political correctness. Nevertheless, reopen the subject I must, for the salvation of millions (and their eternal destination) is at stake.

---

* http://lcweb2.loc.go/ammem/today/jul20.html#hutchinson; http://loc.go/exhibits/religion/relo1-2.htm, accessed February 18, 2006.

** Harold J. Chadwick, ed., *Foxe's Book of Martyrs: Updated to the 21st Century* (Gainesville, FL: Bridge-Logos, 2001), 285–287.

Now is the time that the truth about water baptism must become clear, for it is primarily the teaching of two modes of water baptism and the value assigned to each that has kept the Church separated for centuries.

> There is one body and one Spirit, just as you were called in one hope of your calling; one Lord, one faith, *one baptism,* one God and Father of all, who is above all, and through all, and in you all.
>
> —Ephesians 4:4–6, emphasis added

Studying the subject of water baptism is important, for the Bible says there are seven doctrines of the faith that we must understand if we are to mature as Christians, one of which, according to Hebrews 6:1–2, is the doctrine of baptisms. If the Bible considers baptism to be as important as eternal judgment and resurrection of the dead, then surely we can take the time to study it, too.

> Therefore, leaving the discussion of the elementary principles of Christ, let us go on to perfection, not laying again the foundation of repentance from dead works and of faith toward God, *of the doctrine of baptisms*, of laying on of hands, of resurrection of the dead, and of eternal judgment.
>
> —Hebrews 6:1–2, emphasis added

Discovering and teaching the one, true baptism will unify the Church that Jesus Christ left here on Earth. This is very important because Jesus' last earthly prayer on the night before He was crucified was for unity in the Church. He asked the Father for unity in the Church so that all could discover that God loves them and desires reconciliation with them. He wanted them to know of God's love so that they could all believe and be brought into the safety of His fold.*

Today, we are alive at an exciting time in history. Surely Jesus is returning soon. The time is now for the Father to grant the dying request of His only Son! Unity will come as denominations restudy baptism and change their church doctrines to agree with the Bible.

Fractures will heal as the whole Church acknowledges and teaches the one baptism of Scripture.

* John 17

2

DOCTRINAL DIVERSITY

THE PROBLEM CAUSED BY having two different water baptisms is bigger than most Christians are willing to admit, if the inquiries on the World Wide Web are any indication. There were 371,000 Web sites with references to baptism in 2001. A more recent check showed the number had grown to nearly twelve million sites!* But when I asked the lady at customer service desk of our local Christian bookstore for books on water baptism, she could find only one thin booklet.

The numbers tell the story. People are longing to know the truth about water baptism. Were they saved or not when they were baptized as infants? And, they wonder if infant baptism is necessary for salvation. They are sensing something is not quite right with the doctrine they have been told will give them eternal salvation.

Some time ago, I was having lunch with a member of our prayer group when a waitress literally stole some papers out from under my nose because they had *baptism* written across the top. We had gotten together to look over and discuss the

* *Google* search engine

material in the manuscript, and I had laid it aside for just a moment while we prepared to order.

As we studied the menus, a waitress approached our table. When she completed writing down our selections, the young lady, barely out of her teens, picked up the menus and then seemed to hesitate just a moment as she glanced over at my manuscript. She thanked us for our orders, set the menus down on my papers, and suddenly swooped everything up and headed for the kitchen.

It all happened so fast. It was my only copy! Summoning another waitress, I quickly told her what had happened and she took off for the kitchen on the run to retrieve the papers.

It wasn't long before the first girl reappeared, papers in hand, tears running down her cheeks. I tried to set her at ease. I told her I didn't think she meant any harm. I even said I didn't think she planned on keeping the manuscript. But she only cried harder, pausing just long enough to blurt out, "Oh, but I did take them on purpose!" And then she told me the following: "It seems I just don't know right from wrong anymore. I was living with my boyfriend and we got pregnant. We want to do what's right for the baby and all and get back into church, but we aren't sure which is the right church anymore."

She said she had been raised Catholic but her boyfriend didn't like attending church anymore. She had taken my papers because she wanted to "find out stuff for the baby." And then she started to cry again.

Seeing her so troubled and because of the events she had related to me, I asked her, "Are you worried about whether God will forgive you?" I thought I could show her in the

Bible what God says about forgiveness, and maybe that would relieve her mind.

But she answered no. "I'm not worried about that," she said, "because my grandma is Pentecostal and she explained salvation to me already. But now she says the Bible also says to be baptized in water to show Jesus that I really meant what I prayed."

The girl went on to explain that she had asked the priest from her church to baptize her, but he had turned her down, saying she had been baptized when she was a baby and that was enough for her. "I just don't know what's right any more," she said, beginning to cry again.

I have not been able to forget how disturbed that young waitress was about what part water baptism should play in being right with God. She had tried to seek out answers from two people she trusted, but she only came away with more confusion because each gave her a different answer. Her problem with the contradicting doctrines of the two branches of the Church is not all that unusual, for strangely enough, a similar incident occurred a short time later that reminded me once again how much pain and turmoil false Church doctrine causes people as they try to know God and go to heaven when they die.

At that time, I had been visiting Orlando, Florida, spending a few days with my husband while he was away on a business trip. We had to take separate flights home and his was later, so he dropped me off at the airport. I entered the plane early and settled in my seat as later passengers boarded. I pulled my Bible out of my carry-on, intending to read while I waited. It was not long before a woman in her mid-seventies entered the plane and started slowly down the aisle. As she passed each row, she carefully examined the numbers on the outside seats.

When she came to my row, she found it matched the number on her ticket, and she stowed her bag under the seat and sat down. Almost immediately, she looked across at me and started to engage me in conversation.

She and her husband had been farmers in Iowa, she volunteered. She was alone now and owned a small condo in Florida. She was on her way to Phoenix, where she and several of her six children were gathering for Thanksgiving the next day. Noting my open Bible, she said she had been raised Methodist but had married a Catholic. She had taken instruction in the Catholic Church before marriage and had signed over her children to be raised in the Catholic faith. None of them had been religious as children, but now two were attending Lutheran churches, one was still Roman Catholic, two had become Mormons, and the last had become a Pentecostal. She said this diversity was threatening to tear her family apart.

"I tell them all roads lead to heaven," she said. "I tell them 'don't talk about religion,' but my Pentecostal son says all roads do not lead to heaven. He tells his brothers and sisters they aren't even going to get there unless they find out what the Bible says about salvation." She sighed, "It's getting so I hate to even go to family gatherings anymore."

I asked her what she believed, and she pondered my question before answering. "To tell you the truth," she finally said, "I don't know. But I'm getting old—*and I need to know*!"

3

CALLED TO WRITE

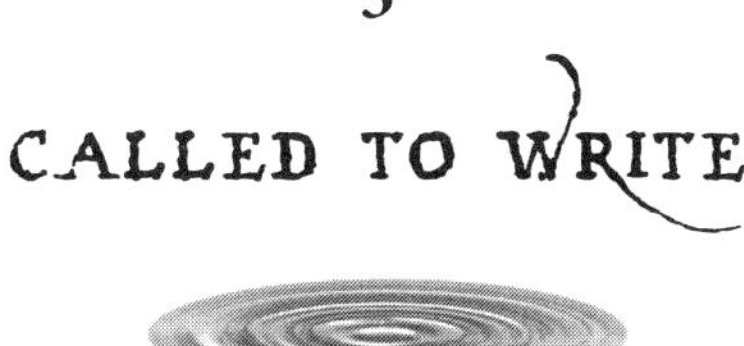

MY RESEARCH INTO THE subject of infant baptism began when a staff member at our five thousand-member Lutheran church asked me to write a twelve-week Bible course for their adult Christian education department. They wanted a class that would study the Holy Spirit and the gifts He brings to the body of Christ. I was asked to help develop the new curriculum because I had written Bible studies before.

At first, I had not been sure whether I wanted to do this. While I found the subject of the Holy Spirit fascinating and had always thought that someday I would like to write a full-length book on the third person of the Trinity, I knew writing on the Holy Spirit would open up the subject of water baptism. I wasn't sure that was a good idea in the Lutheran church we were then attending.

After all those years, I was being confronted with the issue that had caused me so many questions. It did not seem that I could possibly write curriculum on the Holy Spirit and skirt the subject of water baptism. After all, it was the Holy Spirit who empowered Jesus to do His mighty miracles—and it happened at the time of His water baptism.

Because of the part played by the Holy Spirit in the baptismal waters of the River Jordan, the subject would definitely have to be addressed. The students would ask questions about what actually happened to Jesus in water baptism and whether He was immersed or sprinkled. And was something supposed to happen inside of believers today like what happened inside of Jesus on that day? I was concerned because the topic of water baptism is volatile in the Christian Church.

I thought about the story of Jesus' water baptism. John the Baptist had at first refused to baptize Him because He sensed that Jesus was no ordinary man. He somehow knew Jesus had no sin of which He needed to repent, and John's baptism was a baptism of repentance. God had sent him to offer to the citizens of Israel a baptism for the remission of sin. But why, John wondered, would Jesus want to take part in such a water baptism when He was without sin?

Yet Jesus stood firm. He told John it was necessary for Him to do this so He could "fulfill all righteousness." John did not understand, but he agreed to baptize Jesus after telling Him that it was *he* who needed to be baptized by *Him*.*

There are only a very few things about Christ's life that appear in all four Gospels, but John's baptism of repentance is one of them. All four writers shout the fact that Jesus came for the very purpose of baptizing believers with—believe it or not—the Holy Spirit!** It was to be the major event, so I knew it must have been a very important event to God the Father and God the Holy Spirit.

So, I decided it must be important enough to me, too, that

---

* Matthew 3:13–15

** Matthew 3:11

I would boldly examine it in the curriculum I was writing. I said yes to developing the curriculum, and having made that decision, I spent a year doing research before I began writing. My goal was to show that the Holy Spirit was equally active throughout both the Old Testament and the New Testament.

I wanted to show this to students through incidents taken directly from the Bible. That way, they would understand that they could embrace the Holy Spirit and not think He was some strange and recent idea thought up by man's imagination. I wanted them to welcome the Holy Spirit's ministry to and through them.

After all, God had sent the Holy Spirit to believers as a helper and a friend, according to the New Testament book of John. (See John 14:16.) I would show them how important the Holy Spirit was to Jesus and how carefully He explained the benefits of the Holy Spirit to His disciples. In The Amplified Version of the Bible, we are given a good, in-depth description of Jesus' explanation of the benefits of the Holy Spirit, which He had already experienced in His own life.

> However, I am telling you nothing but the truth when I say it is profitable (good, expedient, advantageous) for you that I go away. Because if I do not go away, the Comforter (Counselor, Helper, Advocate, Intercessor, Strengthener, Standby) will not come to you [into close fellowship with you]; but if I go away, I will send Him to you [to be in close fellowship with you].
>
> —John 16:7, AMP

The Holy Spirit was no Johnny-come-lately, and I wanted my students to know that He helped God all throughout the creation process, even garnishing the skies for our enjoyment of the heavens we see each day. I decided I would start with the very first story in the Bible—that of Creation—as found in the first chapter of Genesis. I would make people aware that God had said, "Let *Us* make man in *Our* image" (v. 26, emphasis added).

I planned to point out that the Hebrew word for "God" used in that verse was the word *Elohim*, a plural noun, implying that the word, *God*, in that passage includes the Father, Son, and Holy Spirit aspect of the Godhead, the "one God in three persons" concept that is central to today's Christianity. Then they would know that the Holy Spirit is an extension of God, not a separate entity, just as is Jesus. That is why we can say we serve a single God even though the Father God was never alone in His approach to man.

Soon I finished my research and was ready to write one session a week. My husband and I would then, on weekends, use a team-teaching approach to present this material to a pilot class of twelve. Doing it was great fun, and the group was unusually enthusiastic. We got instant feedback; the students insisted they had never grown so fast spiritually.

But the euphoria soon came to an end, and, of course, the trouble started the week I began writing about water baptism. I looked up the word *baptism* in my *Strong's Exhaustive Concordance of Bible Words*, which lists every word in the Bible and the verses in which they are included. There I found more than a hundred verses referring to six different baptisms.

I gave that week's curriculum the title Baptisms! Baptisms! Baptisms! as I pondered this unexpected development.

I found there were more than one hundred verses that referred to baptisms. As I looked each up in my Bible, I saw they referred to six different baptisms; more if one considered household baptisms (Acts 2:38 baptisms that occurred in one family at one time) or baptizing the dead (so-named because those publicly baptized [Acts 2:38] often literally took their lives in their hands). A contemporary example might be seen in the Middle East today when a Muslim converts to Christianity and is publicly baptized, often resulting in his death.*

Analyzing the situation, I soon realized the six baptisms fell into a neat pattern of three old covenant and three new covenant baptisms.** The first two of the old covenant baptisms were Noah's baptism, when the floodwaters covered over and drowned Noah's enemies while he and his family continued on in safety in the ark;*** and Moses' baptism, in which the waters of the Red Sea covered over and drowned the enemies of the children of Israel while they continued on in safety.****

The third old covenant baptism was John's baptism of repentance for the remission of sin.***** Technically, John's baptism was a bridge between the ending of the old covenant and the beginning of the new covenant. Though written about in the New Testament, it is still an old covenant baptism because Jesus had not yet shed His blood, which would ratify the new

---

* See *The Hebrew-Greek Key Word Bible*, P. 1696; *A Dictionary of the Bible*, pp. 74-75; *Funk & Wagnalls New Standard Bible Dictionary,* p. 94.

** Acts 2:38

*** 1 Peter 3:20–21

**** 1 Corinthians 10:1–2

***** Matthew 3:1–11

and better covenant. I set those baptisms aside as not being immediately relevant to the new covenant believer.

There were also three new covenant baptisms. They were (1) a water baptism into the name of Jesus Christ, (2) a baptism of the Holy Spirit, and (3) a baptism of fire. All three baptisms can be found in the following verse:

> Repent, and let every one of you be baptized in the name of Jesus Christ for the remission of sins; and you shall receive the gift of the Holy Spirit.
>
> —Luke 3:16

The first baptism mentioned in that verse is an after-conversion water baptism, the second is the Holy Spirit baptism, and the third is a baptism of fire—the last two being irretrievably linked together in the book of Luke. When one receives the Holy Spirit, one must be prepared for both extraordinary joy and fiery trials.

> I indeed baptize you with water; but One mightier than I is coming, whose sandal strap I am not worthy to loose. He will baptize you with the Holy Spirit and fire.
>
> —Acts 2:38

But I could not find the water baptism for which I was looking, the one our denomination taught. I simply could not find any indication in the Bible that babies were baptized—only repentant people with converted hearts.*

* Matthew 18:3

Though I had read all the verses in the Bible that referred to baptism, there did not seem to be any biblical way to validate infant baptism. In our church, this is very serious. Members are taught from a young age that they were saved as babies when they were baptized. Now I was left without any evidence about our church's baptism to complete that weekend's curriculum.

I had been working late at church all that week trying to find Scripture to use for the weekend's lesson. I finally had no recourse but to call our pastor at home for help. Surely he would have studied the subject in seminary and could give me some answers.

When he picked up the phone that evening, I explained who I was and that I was having difficulty finding Scripture to verify infant baptism. But first, I asked whether he really believed in infant baptism. I did this respectfully, because he was the one who conducted the Sunday morning baptismal ceremonies at our church. I had noticed that although he gave the same verse every Sunday, it referred to small children but not to water baptism. It was Jesus' response to His disciples question about which of them would be greatest in the kingdom of heaven.

True, a little child is mentioned in that verse, but it was, in reality, addressing the need to have a converted heart in order to become innocent and childlike so one could enter the kingdom of heaven: "Assuredly, I say to you, unless you are converted and become as little children, you will by no means enter the kingdom of heaven" (Matt. 18:3).

The pastor assured me in no uncertain terms, however, that he did indeed believe in infant baptism. In fact, he said, his assurance grew year by year, "even though it cannot be found in the Bible, *per se*." He told me, "This is because it is hidden in Scripture. But if you will do a word search on Old Testament circumcision, you will find plenty of information to validate a baptism of infants."

He added that this is because infant baptism is a "thinly-veiled" type of New Testament circumcision. He explained this was true because the ritual of physical circumcision "saved" under the old covenant. "For this reason," he said, "the ritual of infant baptism can save under the new covenant, because it is a thinly-veiled type of New Testament circumcision."

Then he added one more thing before hanging up. He told me that I should also look up all the New Testament passages that refer to household baptisms. "With these two things—circumcision and household baptisms," he assured me, "you will have more than enough material to finish the curriculum on baptism for this weekend's class."

He hung up, and once again I started by looking up Bible verses with the words *circumcise, circumcised*, or *circumcision* in them. As I began to read the verses, I was shocked to discover that the Bible does not teach that circumcision saves at all. In fact, it teaches that if we believe that circumcision saves, we will fall from grace.

> Indeed, I, Paul, say to you that if you become circumcised, Christ will profit you nothing. And I testify again to every man who becomes circumcised that he is a debtor to keep the whole law. You have become estranged from Christ, you who attempt to be justified by law; you have fallen from grace.
>
> —Galatians 5:2–4

I looked up even more verses containing the words *circumcise* and *circumcision* in them and discovered that, contrary to what my denomination teaches, the New Testament does not say that circumcision saves. More than one book of the Bible warns that we are not to believe the ritual of circumcision is a part of new covenant salvation.

> For what does the Scripture say? "Abraham believed God, and it [not circumcision] was accounted to him for righteousness."
>
> —Romans 4:3

And then:

> How then was it accounted? While he was circumcised, or uncircumcised? Not while circumcised, but while uncircumcised.
>
> —Romans 4:10

As I began to study the ritual of Old Testament circumcision, I learned that Abraham, the patriarch of our faith, was not saved by the ritual of circumcision either. He was not even circumcised until twenty-five years after God called him righteous solely because of his faith.* His circumcision, according to God, was to be a sign of the faith he already had.** Therefore, I had to conclude that the information I had been given was wrong. I had to conclude that if the original circumcision of the old covenant did not save the father of our faith, then a

* Genesis 15:6

** Genesis 17:9–14

thinly-veiled type of that circumcision—as my denomination calls infant baptism—would not save either.

Concerned, I started researching the second clue my pastor had given me, that of household baptisms. First of all, I wanted to see if Scripture said—in words—that infants were included when whole households were baptized; or if it stated that all who were baptized were first believers. I decided my criteria for whether someone was a believer would be if they listened to the gospel as it was preached and then consciously made a decision to believe based on what they had heard.

Because the Philippian jailer's household is most often mentioned as sterling proof that babies were included in household baptisms, I decided to start there. I began by carefully examining the following verses. The key, I felt, lay in the last verse, where it clearly states that the jailer's entire household believed before they were baptized.

> But at midnight Paul and Silas were praying and singing hymns to God, and the prisoners were listening to them. Suddenly there was a great earthquake, so that the foundations of the prison were shaken; and immediately all the doors were opened and everyone's chains were loosed. And the keeper of the prison, awaking from sleep and seeing the prison doors open, supposing the prisoners had fled, drew his sword and was about to kill himself. But Paul called with a loud voice, saying, "Do yourself no harm, for we are all here." Then he called for a light, ran in, and fell down trembling before Paul and Silas. And he brought them out

> and said, "Sirs, what must I do to be saved?" So they said, "Believe on the Lord Jesus Christ, and you will be saved, you and your household." Then they spoke the word of the Lord to him and to all who were in his house. And he took them the same hour of the night and washed their stripes. And immediately he and all his family were baptized. Now when he had brought them into his house, he set food before them; and he rejoiced, having believed in God with all his household.
>
> —Acts 16:25–34

The Bible could not be clearer in the first four examples of baptism, one of which is the above-mentioned jailer's household. In all four examples, it clearly emphasizes that those who were baptized first had personal faith.

- The jailer's household were all believers before they were baptized. (See Acts 16:16–34, esp. v. 34.)
- In Cornelius's household, all who were baptized were believers. (See Acts 10:1–48, esp. vv. 1, 44.)
- Stephanas' household were all believers. (See 1 Corinthians 16:15.)
- Regarding the household of Crispus, all believed. (See Acts 18:8.)

The fifth example is less clear. It is the story of Lydia, a seller of purple, and her household. The apostle Paul and his entourage went to Philippi, the main city in Macedonia. There they stayed for several days. On the Sabbath, he went down to the riverbank, where he found several devout women who habitually gathered for prayer on that day. The group included Lydia and her household.

Already believers in God, they listened when Paul taught the gospel of Christ. He evidently explained the need to take part in water baptism to prove one's faith in Christ was sincere, for Lydia and her household responded to his preaching by being baptized.

> And on the Sabbath day we went out of the city to the riverside, where prayer was customarily made; and we sat down and spoke to the women who met there. Now a certain woman named Lydia heard us. She was a seller of purple from the city of Thyatira, who worshiped God. The Lord opened her heart to heed the things spoken by Paul. And when she and her household were baptized, she begged us, saying, "If you have judged me to be faithful to the Lord, come to my house and stay." So she persuaded us.
>
> —Acts 16:13–15

These verses state that women were present that day. At the same time, they do not mention babies or men or children being present, so it would be presumptuous to assume that babies were present at Lydia and her household's riverside baptism. We know that Lydia listened and responded to the gospel, but Scripture is silent about her household. We can assume this to be true but we can't be sure. Therefore, it cannot be stated as actual fact.

However, it appears that our denomination's salvation doctrine lies in the silence of Scripture—the noninformation found in the example of Lydia's household—that gives infant baptism denominations the license to teach their members that they were saved when they were baptized as babies. As for me, I was back where I started. Clearly circumcision could not be used as proof of infant baptism, and household baptisms gave no concrete evidence for a baptism of infants. It did not seem possible that a Christian denomination would risk the eternal damnation of their members by teaching something that could not be found in the Bible. This bothered me.

I decided to take a year out of my life to attend a Lutheran Bible school affiliated with our church. I thought, "Surely a Lutheran school will study the subject of infant baptism, and I will find the answers for which I am looking."

4

BACK TO SCHOOL

I SIGNED UP FOR SCHOOL that same fall. During the coming year, I would sit under more than twenty of the most respected Lutheran teachers and pastors in our area. The instructors were interesting and the school intense, as it studied every book in the Old and New Testaments in two years.

As the year went on, I began to notice something unusual that was happening. In most of my classes, the teachers would be teaching their assigned subjects, when suddenly they would abandon their notes and energetically exhort the students to accept infant baptism. There, for a period of just a few minutes, we would be heartily admonished to believe the Lutheran doctrine of salvation, which included infant baptism. Then, just as suddenly, the subject would be dropped and they would return to their classroom assignment.

I watched this happen time after time. I also noticed that no Bible verses were ever given to support their stand. I, too, had been unable to find even one reference to validate baby baptisms, so I would raise my hand to ask if they had chapter and verse to back up what we were being taught. I was invariably given the same two responses that our pastor had given me—Old Testament circumcision and New Testament household baptisms. Of course, they would become offended when I asked for proof.

I became more and more concerned about this, so one afternoon I made an appointment with the head of our school to talk to him about my concerns. He seemed anxious to meet with me, too. In fact, a class on what to do with divisive people using Titus as a textbook had shown up as newly-inserted school curriculum.

So after class the next day, I went to my appointment at his office. I knocked on his open door and he stood up and kindly motioned me to a chair. I wasted no time launching into my story. I told him of my concern that the worldwide Church had two very different methods for getting to heaven, and I told him about writing the twelve-week study course for our church and being unable to validate the claims our church makes for salvation through a baptism of infants.

I mentioned Lydia's household. I told him the non-information in that passage was as close as I could come to backing up our denomination's stand on infant baptism but that my concern was that if the silence of Scripture can be used as proof, then anyone could add anything they wanted to Church doctrine as long as the Bible did not specifically disallow it.

"For example," I said, "they could take the Scripture where it says that Peter, Jesus' disciple, was standing beside the fire in the high priest's courtyard the night before Jesus' crucifixion. Using the same criteria as was used to prove infant baptism, they could add to it by saying that Peter was roasting hotdogs and marshmallows over that fire and selling them to the crowd as they warmed their hands."

I told him no one could contradict this new bit of information about Peter's entrepreneurial efforts if the silence of Scripture was all that was necessary to prove such a statement was true. I finished by saying, "This is how false religions get started."

The old gentleman just sat there for a long time after I finished. He didn't say anything. I began to get nervous and thought my example was too silly for him to respond. But finally he spoke up. "I, too, once questioned infant baptism," he said, "but I saw the light, so to speak." And he urged me to do the same.

And maybe I would have—just to please him—if he had not dropped the next bombshell. He then said, "I was never ordained, you know."

Well, of course I did not know that. He is respected as one of the genuine patriarchs in our church and he is the founder of our Bible school for laypeople. Everyone calls him "Reverend," and he has lead numerous mission trips. I had always assumed he was ordained, but I had to admit it was not something I had thought about.

I could see that what he was telling me was hard for him, but he continued. He said that after taking all the coursework and graduating from a Lutheran seminary, the Lutheran denomination refused to ordain him because he was married to a Mennonite woman. I was dumbfounded. I knew his wife. She was a beautiful, kind, and godly Christian woman. How could it be that a man like him couldn't be ordained when he was married to someone of as high a Christian character as she?

He said that many years ago there had been some trouble

between the Lutherans and the Mennonites over infant baptism. My ears perked up. He said the Mennonites even today are worried that the Lutheran and Catholic Churches will start persecuting them anew if they recognize who they are.

I tried to get more information from him, but he wouldn't say anymore. I knew even what he had said was hard for him. But I was shocked. Even then, I really did not understand. The idea of one church persecuting another church was so foreign to me.

Little did I know that the time would come when I would find answers to my questions through a three-inch thick, ancient, and obscure book that I found in a little Mennonite museum in Canada. This book, *Martyrs Mirror*, lists a multitude of men, women, and children whose blood was spilled all over Europe by the Roman Catholic Church and, later, by some of the founders of Protestant churches as well because they did not believe infant baptism was biblical, refused to baptize their own babies, and told others.

As I left the founder's office that day, I had many things to ponder, but I knew quitting my search for the truth was not one of them. In fact, I desired more than ever to find out why the Church has two branches, two baptisms and two different ways of salvation.

There was no way I could stop my search now.

5

THE ANSWER COMETH

DAY BY DAY, I continued to search for answers. One day, after a particularly harsh rebuke from a visiting pastor because of my questions, I decided not to join the other students at coffee break. Frankly, I was feeling foolish. My questions were making me unpopular with both students and staff. Even I knew I seemed divisive at times, even though, if the truth were known, I really wanted to get along just like everybody else.

That day I walked toward the back of the room with a heavy heart. The threat always nagging at my mind, of course, was that if I did not stop asking questions, I would get kicked out of school and embarrass my husband.

We were friends with people on staff. The groomsman at our wedding was one of the ruling elders on the church council. My husband and I were teachers at the church. Our daughter attended their day school. By now, my curriculum was being used in several new classes. I didn't want to offend and, to be honest, the temptation to drop the whole subject was continually in the back of my mind.

As I paced back and forth at the back of the room that day, I was contemplating all the trouble I was getting into when, suddenly, God spoke to my heart. It wasn't audible, but it was very distinct. No one else heard it but me, but on the inside I was clearly impressed with these words:

> Neither baptism nor un-baptism matters, but adding it to the finished work of the cross nullifies it.

I was surprised—God had spoken to me! The words seemed to reverberate inside as I turned them over in my mind. True, I had been praying to Him but I had not expected Him to answer me—at least not in that way.

At first, it was not clear to me what God was trying to say. What did the words, "Neither baptism nor un-baptism matters" mean? Could churches baptize any way they wanted? Were they free to baptize infants or adults, believers or the unconverted, according to their own discretion?

And I wondered how believing in water baptism could make one lose the benefits of the cross? Yet the word God had just given me said that making baptism necessary for salvation would nullify the benefits Christ had won for us on the cross.

I continued to ponder the words I had heard, and the Lord brought to my mind a Bible verse I had memorized years ago. I compared the two, noticing how very similar in meaning they were, except that the Bible verse referred to a ritual of circumcision and the word the Lord had given me had referred to a ritual of baptism.

> Neither circumcision nor uncircumcision avails anything, but faith working through love.
>
> —GALATIANS 5:6

I asked the Lord for understanding, and slowly it began to dawn on me the seriousness of what He had shown me. In fact, it almost took my breath away, for I remembered a Sunday school class taught by the pastor of a church my husband and I had previously attended. The class was entitled Great Doctrines of the Church.

The Sunday we joined the class, the pastor had chosen to teach about an error that had gotten into the early Church that was so serious that it caused men to lose their salvation. He said contemporary historians called it the *dreaded* Heresy of the Judaizer—it was the worst because it was the most subtle.

The error had come about because some false brethren from Judea had insisted that the apostle Paul teach that even under the new covenant, one must be circumcised in order to be saved. The apostle refused to preach this, saying that a ritual did not save and that they would fall from grace if they put their faith in a ritual.*

The pastor, however, assured his class that the Jerusalem Council had dealt with the Heresy of the Judaizer long ago. He said it was no longer a problem for the Christian Church.

But was he wrong? Had a ritual of infant baptism merely been substituted for the ritual of circumcision?

---

* Acts 15

6

SEVEN LETTERS SENT

SCHOOL WAS ALMOST OVER for that year when I made my startling discovery. One of the last courses we had that spring was a class taught by a retired missionary entitled World Missions. The elderly man dearly loved the stories of Martin Luther and the early Lutheran Church. He described his great disappointment in not having enough class time to dig deeper into the great Protestant Reformation of the 1500s so that we could see how much Martin Luther had affected history.

He said that we, as Christians, had a responsibility to know the facts and understand the events that surrounded the great Reformation. He challenged us to set aside time to do research on the issues. He said both public and seminary libraries contain much information on those times and that it was still important even though it happened a long time ago.

This opened my eyes to the fact that there was a whole body of literature available having to do with the roots of my denomination—a place where I could go to research ancient Church history and learn how baptismal regeneration through infant baptism entered Church doctrines. Excited, I resolved to spend my whole summer, if necessary, researching the

Reformation and the part Martin Luther played in it. Little did I know then that I was beginning a decade-long search.

In the beginning, I only wanted to know why Martin Luther had turned away from his pre-Reformation stand on salvation by faith alone and returned to the Roman Catholic belief in infant baptism (baptismal regeneration). But as time went on, I saw that the integrity of our Church was at stake.

During this time, the leadership at our church was pondering whether or not to remain under the covering of the ELCA. The leadership had just released a controversial position paper on human sexuality that had many churches belonging to that organization in an uproar.

This was not the first time they had taken nonbiblical stands about Church issues, and for this reason, our church was seeking God to see if they should remain under the covering of the ELCA as a light and a conscience or if they should get out. To help in making this decision, the pastor invited input from the congregation.

Because of the Bible verse that says a good tree cannot bear bad fruit and a bad tree cannot bear good fruit,* I had begun to wonder what it was in the roots of the Lutheran Church that was causing such bad fruit to emanate from ELCA leadership. Little did I know then that by searching for these roots I would also be led to the answers on infant baptism for which I was seeking.

By going to several different libraries, I was able to find the facts summarized in these chapters. A Baptist seminary and a Lutheran seminary both provided information. The

* Matthew 7:17–18

University of Minnesota library and a secular public research library were also used. My greatest find, though, came from an opportunity I had to do research in the library of a college on the East Coast whose library houses one of the finest collections of early Christian documents and books in the world.

As my research progressed, I wrote letters to my church telling them of the things I was uncovering as I searched for the roots of our denomination. With each letter I would think I had uncovered enough, but then I would find one more startling revelation and end up writing one more letter and sending it off.

At first, these letters were only for the eyes of our pastors and church council members, but as time has passed, I have come to realize that this information is even more relevant for the body of Christ today than when the letters were written a few short years ago. I have been able to uncover many things long hidden because of the prayer and fasting of our church and because of the faithful weekly prayer group that gathered together and prayed for me during this time of research. Things hidden for generations in secular and seminary libraries were uncovered.

It was during this time that I discovered more about the ancient Heresy of the Judaizer.

7

ANCIENT HERESY UNCOVERED

One of the first things I uncovered as I began my research was that, at the time when the New Testament was being written, false teaching was already trying to enter the Church. One error in particular would be so serious that half the world's churches have been duped by it. Theologians call it the dreaded Heresy of the Judaizer.

The pastor at our previous church had taught on the subject of the Heresy of the Judaizer, but it took reading and rereading the book of Galatians many times at the prompting of the Lord before I saw the connection between my church's infant baptism ritual and the Old Testament ritual of circumcision. I saw that because our denomination teaches that infant baptism is a thinly-veiled type of circumcision, the Heresy of the Judaizer also applied to our church and other infant baptism denominations.

The apostle Paul had warned the early Church that men from within the Church itself would bring in a devastating error: "Therefore take heed to yourselves and to all the flock, among which the Holy Spirit has made you overseers, to shepherd the church of God which He purchased with His own blood. For I know this, that after my departure savage wolves will come in among you, not sparing the flock. Also from among yourselves men will rise up, speaking perverse things, to draw away the disciples after themselves. Therefore watch, and remember that for three years I did not cease to warn everyone night and day with tears" (Acts 20:28–31).

He told the churches of Galatia, "I marvel that you are turning away so soon from Him who called you in the grace of Christ, to a different gospel, which is not another; but there are some who trouble you and want to pervert the gospel of Christ. But even if we, or an angel from heaven, preach any other gospel to than what we have preached to you, let him be accursed" (Gal. 1:6–7).*

The heresy Paul was referring to was the Heresy of the Judaizer. By putting their faith in a ritual instead of the blood Christ shed for sinners on the cross, this error was canceling out true salvation by faith alone—which is given as the only way to heaven in both the Old Testament** and the New Testament.***

Some Jews from Judea did not understand that it was prophesied in the Old Testament that the ritual of physical circumcision was to become a spiritual circumcision of the heart under the new covenant. They insisted physical circumcision was necessary for salvation, but putting their faith in a ritual would have caused them to fall from grace.

> Indeed I, Paul, say to you that if you become circumcised, Christ will profit you nothing. And I testify

---

* Galatians 1:6-7

** Genesis 15:6

*** Romans 1:17

> again to every man who becomes circumcised that he is a debtor to keep the whole law. You have become estranged from Christ, you who attempt to be justified by law; you have fallen from grace.
>
> —Galatians 5:2–4

So serious did the early Church consider the Heresy of the Judaizer that the first Church council ever called was convened in Jerusalem to deal with this error. The apostle Peter spoke before the gathering, sharing with the assembled leadership (including Jesus' other disciples) that God had already accepted the Gentiles at Cornelius's house without a ritual.* So, after much discussion, a conclusion was made: the Bible does not say that a ritual is necessary for salvation, and that if one believes that salvation comes through a ritual, he has set aside the grace of God.

> I do not set aside the grace of God; for if righteousness comes through the law [a ritual], then Christ died in vain.
>
> —Galatians 2:21

At that time, a letter was drafted to the churches from the Jerusalem Council that stated that a ritual was not necessary for salvation. It was circulated to all the churches of Galatia and eventually ended up in a book in the New Testament:

> Since we heard that some who went out from us have troubled you with words, unsettling your souls,

* Acts 10

> saying, "You must be circumcised and keep the law"—to whom we gave no such commandment—it seemed good to us, being assembled with one accord, to send chosen men to you with our beloved Barnabas and Paul…who will also report the same things by word of mouth.
>
> —Acts 15:24–25, 27

That should have clinched the matter. The question had been openly discussed. The Church elders and apostles believed they had the mind of the Lord on the matter and had dealt with it decisively. But the Judaizers would not let the matter lie even after those at the Jerusalem Council, composed of Jesus' disciples as well as elders of the Church, had made their joint ruling.

However, the Judaizers continued to interrupt Paul's missionary journeys and physically attacked him because he insisted on preaching that a ritual was not to be a part of new covenant Christianity. When the apostle wrote the New Testament book of Galatians, he found it necessary to teach on this problem again. He said, "O foolish Galatians! Who has bewitched you that you should not obey the truth, before whose eyes Jesus Christ was clearly portrayed among you as crucified? This only I want to learn from you: Did you receive the Spirit by the works of the law, or by the hearing of faith?" (Gal. 3:1–2).

The Judaizer was choosing to keep all of the more than six hundred Old Testament laws perfectly including the ritual of circumcision. By insisting that a ritual was necessary for salvation, they were reverting back to the old covenant (circumcision is a ritual of Old Testament law) for their salvation. The old covenant, however, was no longer in effect because Jesus' blood had ratified the new covenant.

This heresy was only one of the many heresies that would come against Christianity during its first centuries. During those years, in subtle ways, Old Testament Judaism would become as much a threat to the purity of the gospel as would the paganism found in the mystery, goddess religions that covered the Roman Empire at that time.

Both Judaism and the pagan religions considered Christianity an enemy to their old way of doing business. Although there were those from both sides who were drawn to Christianity, there also were those from both groups who wanted Christianity's benefits without completely giving up their old ways. These chose to enter the new Church and take on the Christian name without fully embracing its teachings.

Many heresies would spring up in the young Church as a result of mixing Christian practices with pagan practices. Those from Old Testament Judaism who wanted to keep the ritual of circumcision of infants, believing that circumcision saves, contributed to this error, as did those from the goddess religions who wanted to retain the mystery religions' belief that baptism saves. Together, these two errors would eventually meld into a new ritual of baptizing infants—even calling it a form of Old Testament circumcision.

Thus the Heresy of the Judaizer entered the Christian Church. How very conveniently this new ritual would begin to gain theological acceptance as a thinly-veiled type of Old Testament circumcision, even though it was nothing more than the Judaizers' warmed-over error in believing that circumcision saves recycled into a baptism of infants and expressed through baptismal regeneration.* For those in the Church who accepted this error, the Blood of Christ was immediately made of no effect.

Today theologians still debate on the subject of the heresy of the Judaizer. Some believe that it never materialized and are surprised that a council needed to be called to deal with it. Others believe that it was very serious but that it was effectively dealt with at that time. This can be seen in their critiques of the subject.

John Polhill argues that the Heresy of the Judaizer was very serious. In *Paul and His Letters,* he states that the apostle Paul "was absolutely livid" over the Heresy of the Judaizer. Accusing the Galatians of being foolish for accepting the error, he stated they would pay the penalty on Judgment Day because they were alienating themselves from Christ.**

Robert H. Gundry, in *A Survey of the New Testament,* agrees. He stated that fewer and fewer Gentiles would have converted to Christ if the error had not been addressed.*** Jack W. Hayford, editor of *Hayford's Bible Handbook,* concurs. He believes the heresy of the Judaizer was a serious contradiction of the gospel and in direct opposition to the teaching of salvation by faith alone.**** Merrill F. Unger, ThD, PhD, of *Unger's Bible Dictionary,* flatly stated that the Judaizers were not really Christians at all!*****

---

* Genesis 15–17; Acts 15

** John Polhill, *Paul and His Letters* (Nashville, TN: B & H Publishing Group, 1999), 138.

*** R. H. Gundry, *A Survey of the New Testament*, 318.

**** Jack W. Hayford, *Hayford's Bible Handbook*, 637.

***** Merrill F. Unger, *Unger's Bible Dictionary*, 469.

But the secret that even these learned theologians have missed and that I would also have missed if the Lord had not given me a word was that the Heresy of the Judaizer is not just a long-forgotten theological event in Church history. It is very much present in today's Church. Although the heresy has mutated slightly—from a ritual of circumcision to a ritual of baptism—it is still deceiving much of the Church world today and causing many to go into a godless eternity.

There Heresy of the Judaizer—a belief that one can be saved through a ritual—is not only found in the infant baptism churches. It is also found worldwide in religions, such as Hinduism. The Hindus believe that baptism saves and that they become immortal when they are twice-born through dipping in the Ganges River.*

The belief that baptism saves is also found in cults such as the Latter-Day Saints (Mormon) Church. With Christ as a mere figurehead and Christianity a camouflage, Mormons baptize even dead people, believing they are saved in baptism. They teach that if they do enough good works, including proxy baptism of the dead, they will become a god when they die, marry numerous goddess wives, and have their own planet, which they will populate with multitudes of spirit children.**

Thus, the Heresy of the Judaizer—believing salvation comes through observing a ritual—has led many people into deception.

---

* http://www.asiagrace.com

** Ed Decker, "The Law of Eternal Progression," Saints Alive in Jesus, http://www.saintsalive.com/mormonism/eternalprogression.htm (accessed September 2, 2008). See also Paul Bucknell, "Dangers of Mormon Cult Teachings," Biblical Foundations for Freedom, http://www.foundationsforfreedom.net/Topics/Belief/Mormonism.html (accessed September 2, 2008).

8

LUTHER'S FLIP-FLOP

When Luther finally discovered what Jesus meant when He informed Nicodemus, the rich young ruler, that one must be born again, he was stunned. He wondered that salvation could be that easy. He said the gates of paradise seemed to open up to him when he finally succeeded in grasping the simplicity of the gospel, that "the just shall live by faith" (Rom. 1:17).

Although Luther did not label his experience being born again, he had the same experience that evangelicals have long claimed.* Although some may frown on the term and prefer to call it simply "Luther's tower experience," one thing all can agree: he had uncovered the biblical way of salvation long hidden by the official state Church of his day.

Luther himself didn't worry about terminology. Every chance he got, he broadcast to the world around him that when he gave up trying to get to heaven through good works and placed himself in the hands of a merciful God, his faith

* John 3:3

that only the blood of Jesus could save had brought reconciliation with God. Peace flooded his soul.*

Luther had come into agreement with the New Testament truth that salvation is by faith alone and not by any works of man, for Romans 1:17 states, "For in it the righteousness of God is revealed from faith to faith; as it is written, the just shall live by faith." And, in Romans 3:28, it says, "Therefore we conclude that a man is justified by faith apart from the deeds of the law."

Faith is also the way of salvation under the old covenant, for it was not Abraham's circumcision that saved him—it was his faith! Habakkuk 2:4 states, "Behold the proud, his soul is not upright in him; but the just shall live by his faith."

Unfortunately, after Luther was reprimanded at the Diet of Worms and a ban was placed on his life, he moved away from his earlier revelation that salvation is by faith alone. Oh, he still mouthed the words, but he taught a different gospel. He taught that baptism saves, baptismal regeneration. The apostle Paul had warned about this. He said that even if an angel from heaven should come preaching a gospel other than the one he and his team were preaching, they would be eternally condemned, because a perverted gospel is no gospel at all.**

As he got older, Luther seemed to forget that his own early years were miserable and full of the knowledge that he was not right with God, even though he had been baptized as a baby. Before the Diet of Worms, he had written many lovely and true things from Scripture. As early as All Saint's Day in

---

* Heiko A. Oberman, *Luther: Man Between God and the Devil* (New Haven, CT: Yale University Press, 1989), 153. See also WAT 6. No.6647; 95, 14–18.

** Galatians 1:6–9

1517, we read of Luther's zeal that the peasants might know the true way of salvation as he had when he had his famous revelation. He was angry at his mother Church, the Roman Catholics, because they were telling the peasants the way to heaven could only be earned through good deeds and buying forgiveness.

So , it was on the eve of Halloween in 1517 that Luther declared he had enough. He marched up to the door of the Wittenberg church and nailed his now-famous Ninety-five Theses to the church door. In it was Luther's call for reformation within his large and rich Church. Later he would write an important paper called "An Address to the Christian Nobility," which gave his opinion on what would happen to those who believed a work or ritual was necessary for salvation.* Although he did not use the contemporary term Heresy of the Judaizer, a term coined much later in theological circles, he described the error by saying that anyone who attempts to become righteous by works will fall from grace.

> From this anyone can clearly see how a Christian man is free from all things and over all things, so that he needs no works to make him righteous and to save him since faith alone confers all these things abundantly. But should he grow so foolish as to presume to become righteous, free, saved, and a Christian by means of some good work, he would in that instant lose faith and all its benefits.**

---

* Galatians 5:2–4

** Martin Luther, "A Treatise on Christian Liberty," *Three Treatises* (Philadelphia, PA: Muhlenberg Press, 1947), 51.

But as time went on, Martin Luther's passion faded. He still shouted against the Roman Catholic Church, calling them names and insisting that salvation was by faith alone, but, in fact, he was back with them doctrinally. He would after that teach through his writings that a ritual is necessary for salvation in addition to Christ's finished work on the cross. Hardly anyone seemed to notice that he had turned away from his reliance on the Blood of Christ as the one and only way to heaven. His actions stopped the Reformation cold.

There were now two sets of his teachings out there, and no one seemed to notice—the one that set the beleaguered peasant free and gave him a converted heart that of salvation by faith alone, and his prior church's teaching that salvation comes through a ritual, the heresy of the Judaizer.

Luther had been deceived. He had failed to complete the task of purifying the mother Church. This was not unusual. It had also happened to certain other godly leaders that had tried to rid their nation of the idolatry that was being practiced within their borders but had failed. God acknowledged that their hearts were right, but they failed to do the full counsel of God.

Example 1

> Asa did what was right in the eyes of the Lord, as did his father David. And he banished the perverted persons from the land, and removed all the idols that his fathers had made. Also he removed Maachah his grandmother from being queen mother, because she had made an obscene image of Asherah...But the high places were not

> removed. Nevertheless Asa's heart was loyal to the Lord all his days.
>
> —1 Kings 15:11–14

Example 2

> And he [Amaziah] did what was right in the sight of the Lord, yet not like his father David; he did everything he as his father Joash had done. However, the high places were not taken away, and the people still sacrificed and burned incense on the high places.
>
> —2 Kings 14:3–4

Example 3

> Jehoshaphat...walked in all the ways of his father Asa. He did not turn aside from them, doing what was right in the eyes of the Lord. Nevertheless the high places were not taken away, for the people offered sacrifices and burned incense on the high places.
>
> —1 Kings 22:41, 43

Seeing these scriptural examples of godly men who were blinded to the need to tear down the places where idolatry was being practiced in their land and thus failed to complete their task shows the subtlety with which Satan can implant or suggest a slight variation from truth, which will eventually ruin a whole nation or church. These Old Testament kings attempted to purge their nation but failed to get rid of all the places where it was practiced. This eventually led their nation back into idolatry.

That is what happened to Martin Luther. He fell into the same trap as others before him. Before the Reformation, he preached loudly and clearly that salvation is by faith alone. Later, he reversed himself. In place of "saved by faith," he allowed infant baptism and "baptism saves" to be written into Lutheran Church doctrine, just as it had been for centuries in the Roman Catholic Church. Thus, the Heresy of the Judaizer would spread into the Protestant daughter churches that accepted infant baptism.

Martin Luther had fallen victim to the wiles of the dreaded Heresy of the Judaizer, and like everything else he did, he wholeheartedly embraced it.

> The baptismal service was also translated into German, for Luther wished to make the parents of those baptized aware of the importance of this sacrament, by means of which the infant became regenerated, was delivered from the devil, sin, and death' and was made a member of the Christian communion of saints.*

A contemporary of Luther's, John Agricola, noted this discrepancy and brought it to Luther's attention—and to the attention of the other Reformation leaders. This made Luther angry, and he threatened to put a ban on Agricola's life similar to the one the Roman Catholic Church had placed on his life at the Diet of Worms. This meant anyone could kill him on

* Harold J. Grimm, *The Reformation Era* (New York: Macmillan, 1973), 126.

sight and at will, without any civic or, supposedly, eternal penalty.

This pronouncement could have meant Agricola's death, had he not fled the country before Luther could put his threat into action.

> A little later, the controversy with Johann Agricola would produce the first differentiation between the Young Luther (whom Agricola supported) and the Old Luther (who seemed to Agricola to be in opposition to the young Luther).*

Few modern historians have noted this flip-flop. Those who do label Martin Luther's early teachings of salvation by faith alone as the work of the *young* Luther and his later teachings, those of salvation by baptismal regeneration, as those of the *old* Luther. Today's Lutheran Church carries the teachings of the old Luther, although the cliché "salvation by faith alone" is often heard on Sunday mornings.

The Heresy of the Judaizer can be clearly seen in the *Lutheran Book of Worship* where it says clearly that in the waters of infant baptism today's children are reborn.** The doctrinal change to "saved by infant baptism" was slipped into Lutheran Church doctrine in place of "saved by faith." This change did not originate with Luther but was penned by his best friend and longtime associate, Philip Melanchthon.

Philip Melanchthon is known as *the* Lutheran theologian

---

* Bernhard Lohse, *Martin Luther* (Philadelphia, PA: Fortress Press, 1986), 202.

** Inter-Lutheran Commission on Worship, *The Lutheran Book of Worship* (Minneapolis, MN: Augsburg Publishing House, 1978), 121.

in today's seminaries because he wrote most of the doctrine of the Lutheran Church. He inserted "baptism saves" into a doctrinal paper he wrote for a special meeting called between the Catholic and the Lutheran Churches. The purpose of this meeting was to search for common ground upon which to reconcile.

The paper Melanchthon wrote for this meeting is familiar to most people today as the Augsburg Confession. The Augsburg Confession, even today, is considered practically the bible of Lutheran doctrine. In this document, Melanchthon replaced Luther's famous Reformation-starting revelation of salvation by faith alone, with "baptism saves." Many think Melanchthon did this in an effort to curry the favor of the Roman Catholic Church, with whom he secretly hoped to reunite.*

Another possible reason why Melanchthon put baptism saves in the Augsburg Confession is because he was deeply involved in astrology, and baptismal regeneration and astrology run hand in hand. Luther was aware of Melanchthon's involvement with astrology but seemed unaware of the deception it would bring into the new church he was starting.

Luther chided him on his dependence on astrology. He thought it was humorous that Melanchthon would not make even minor decisions without consulting his horoscope. For example, one time just before Luther's death, Melanchthon

* Theodore G. Tappert, *The Book of Concord* (Minneapolis, MN: Augsburg Publishing House, 1959), 13.

delayed their return home even though Luther was not feeling well until his horoscope lined up with their travel plans.*

It was because Melanchthon relied on astrology—not the Bible—that he wanted to keep baptismal regeneration as the theology of the any church in which he took part. Of Greek descent himself, Melanchthon was a professor of Greek and Roman at the University of Wittenberg and was immersed in Greek culture, history, and languages, as well as being thoroughly steeped in the goddess religions of Greek mythology, which rely on baptismal regeneration.**

Because Philip Melanchthon has gained the reputation of being the Lutheran theologian in contemporary seminaries today because he wrote more of the Lutheran Church doctrine than did Martin Luther, it is time to examine the doctrine selected for it way back in the 1500s. This will allow members of that church (and other infant baptism churches) to determine whether the things they are being taught today line up with what the New Testament says. Otherwise, we don't have a Church; we just have one more world religion.

The belief system of any cult is accepted by its members because they do not understand the truth about God's blood covenant, nor do they understand the importance of the shed blood of Jesus Christ. Many seek peace with God but lack doctrinal foundations because they have no basic road map to follow. This makes them prime targets for facsimiles of Christianity.

---

* H. G. Haile, *Luther* (Princeton, NJ: Princeton University Press, 1983), 215; Oberman, 330. See also WAT 5. No. 5368, Summer 1540; K. Martin Luther's Werke: Kritsche Gesamtausgabe Tischreden (Table Talk) Vols. 1–6 (Weimar, 1912-21).

** Haile, 215; Oberman, 330.

These religions look authentic, and may even have Christ as a figurehead, but they deny the saving power of His blood. The Lutheran Church (and other infant baptism denominations) do not wish to fall into the same category as these false religions. Therefore, it is necessary to correct any false teachings that do not line up with the word of God.

We need to be as the Bereans in the New Testament.* Paul commended them as being more noble than their brethren because, although they eagerly listened to his teaching, when they went home, they searched the Scriptures to see for themselves if what he was teaching was in the Bible. (They only had the Old Testament at that time.)

Paul was not offended by their checking up on him even though he wrote most of the New Testament. He knew he was teaching truth and so had no need to be defensive about what they might find. Their care so they were not led astray with deceptive teaching is why he called the Bereans "more noble" than others.**

Neither can we be afraid of the truth. A high place of idolatry has been left in the denomination started by Martin Luther, and it has spread. We need to examine Luther's teachings and be free to teach the truth to our children without fear of offending his memory. Eternal destinies are at stake.

By making infant baptism equally necessary for salvation as is Christ's shed blood on the cross, this ritual has been elevated to the same level as Jesus' sacrifice. As a result, many

---

* Acts 17:11

** Acts 17:10–11

people believe they were saved when they were baptized as a baby.

But the Bible says that if we put our hope for salvation in a ritual, we will fall from grace.*

---

* Galatians 5:2–4

9

NOAH, THE GODDESS RELIGIONS, AND INFANT BAPTISM

JUST AS IT WAS actually quite easy to prove that circumcision does not save and that infant baptism is not found in the Bible, it is equally easy to prove that the belief that "baptism saves" did not originate in the Bible but instead comes out of the occult.

Interestingly enough, the doctrine of baptismal regeneration (baptism saves) has left a paper trail. Many might guess that if its origins could be uncovered at all, it would lead back to the Tower of Babel, for it was at that time that God efficiently divided the people through changing their languages (all without bloodshed), thus breaking their premature drive for one-world unity.* And so it was that God called a halt to what the people were doing so they were no longer able to do all they imagined. Thus, the nations began by the hand of God.

But the origins of the belief that baptism saves can be traced back even further in time than the Tower of Babel to the time of Noah and the great Flood.** There are those who scoff at the possibility of such a major occurrence as a flood covering the

* Genesis 11:1–11

** Genesis 6-9

whole world. However, there is much scientific evidence that the flood really occurred; even remnants of the ark have been sighted and procured. Archeologists dig up fossils showing the sudden demise of animals caught in a state of catastrophe as rain began to fall.

A professor at a nearby college routinely scoffed at Christianity in his "Developing a Philosophy of Life" class. Noah and the Flood story was one of his major targets. The Bible, he would say at the beginning of each semester, is just a book of myths like those found in all other world religions. According to him, it was nothing more than folklore. He pointed out that almost all world religions and literature contain some version of a flood story which, in his worldview, made Noah nothing special.

I was in class one day when he began expounding this opinion. A new student's hand shot up. "Sir," the question was asked, "have you considered the possibility that the flood story might be true—that where there is so much smoke, maybe there really was a fire?"

The prepared student then began to read a footnote from the Amplified Bible. It said that in 1606, a man named P. Jansen of Hoorn, Holland, had produced a model of the ark fashioned after the pattern God gave Noah in Genesis 6:14–16.*

The discovery was made that the pattern for the ark that God gave Noah was wonderfully seaworthy. The vessel was light, waterproof, comfortable, well-ventilated and perfectly planned to be large enough to accommodate the original land animals as well as four couples for the duration of the

* KJV-Amplified Holy Bible: Parallel Bible (Grand Rapids, MI: Zondervan, 1995), 10.

Flood and the drying out period that followed. In fact, it could carry one-third more cargo than any other ship of similar proportions.

According to the *Registry of Shipping, World Almanac*,* Jansen's model of the ark revolutionized shipbuilding and the world's navies. After 1609 when the model was made, ocean-going ships began to be patterned after the biblical rendering of the blueprint God gave Noah to build the ark, for it was beautifully designed and well adapted for floating.

The design of the world's ships only changed again later after vessels became engine-driven and needed a contour designed to be more conducive to speed—a matter of no particular concern to Noah. The professor conceded, and wondered why no one had ever told him that before.

The fact that the biblical rendering of the Noah and the ark story is accurate is no surprise to Bible readers who have long believed that Noah was a real human being and that a flood covered the earth in his day. The Bible teaches that Noah alone was righteous of all the people who were alive on the earth at that time.** So, he was righteous in the eyes of God long before God gave him the instructions that would allow him to build the ark that saved him and his family from destruction when the big Flood came.

Elsewhere in the Bible, Noah is called a preacher.*** It is easy to picture him, the one righteous man among multitudes of wicked men, women, and children, admonishing his fellow citizens to get right with God and to stop their evil ways.

---

* Ibid.

** Genesis 6–8

*** 2 Peter 2:5

But the people would not give heed, and their wickedness so grieved God that He unleashed a gigantic flood that would cover the whole earth and rid it of evil.

God told Noah how to build the huge boat that would save him and his family. Having been given instruction for the ship design, Noah was instructed upon its completion to take on board his wife, three sons and their wives, plus male and female animals of the various species.

God Himself closed the door when Noah's family and the animals were safely on board. When they emerged from the ark many months later, Noah immediately fell on his knees in gratefulness to God for keeping them safe. He hurried to make preparation to build an altar, and there he sacrificed several animals in a burnt offering of thanksgiving.

Generations and centuries went by, and Noah's descendants strived to keep alive the story of their forefather—the one so important that the God of this earth made special arrangements to save his life when all others perished. They told and retold the story of him safely navigating a huge boat through the waters of a flood that ravaged every other creature and every blade of grass.

Unfortunately, they soon forgot that God had been good to their ancestor because and only because of his righteousness. Otherwise he and his family also would have perished like everyone else. They began building Noah up as some great hero who had outwitted God and saved himself. They minimized his righteous walk before God and instead idolized him as a man who had safely navigated the waters of a great flood, a man who they said had successfully contended with God and brought his family to safety when God planned evil upon the whole world.

Intentionally or unintentionally, a religion was born that did not rely on faith in God. The fact that God Himself gave Noah the plan for safekeeping because of his righteousness was soon passed over. His descendents' minds were darkened as they gave credit to Noah for saving himself and seven other souls by craftiness when God sent the great deluge.

Soon a belief in baptismal regeneration emerged. Passing safely through the waters began to be seen as a symbolic way to gain God's favor and go to heaven. A breach developed between man and God, and a false religion was birthed.

In ensuing generations, the myths surrounding Noah's prowess expanded. One example of the retelling of the Noah event is the early *Epic of Gilgamesh* studied worldwide in most college literature classes. On Tablet XI, it relates a flood story similar to Noah's in the Babylonian traditions, in that Utnapishtim plays the part of Noah and, like Noah, survives cosmic destruction by heeding divine orders to build an ark.*

In correlation with the Flood is another phenomena. The result of this strange happening was that there were giants in the land, both before and after the time of Noah. These beings were of enormous size and height. They were descendants of fallen angels who had left their first estate and had gone in to human women, conceiving giant offspring.

> Now it came to pass, when men began to multiply
> on the face of the earth, and daughters were born

* "Noah," *Encyclopedia Britannica* online, http://original.britannica.com/eb/article-9055994/Noah (accessed September 2, 2008).

> to them, that the sons of God saw the daughters of men, that they were beautiful; and they took wives for themselves of all whom they chose....There were giants on the earth in those days, and also afterward, when the sons of God came in to the daughters of men and they bore children to them. Those were the mighty men who were of old, men of renown.
>
> —Genesis 6:1–2, 4

The myths about Noah became intertwined with mankind's fascination with the fathering of these half-angelic/half-human beings. The offspring of these supernatural beings were giants, men of renown, including Goliath, the giant who was killed by the shepherd boy David. Four sons of one giant are mentioned as being killed by David's mighty men. Two of their names were Ishbi-Benob and Saph.*

People were curious about the fact that there had been supernatural beings living in the atmosphere surrounding the earth. Many myths would grow in the imaginations of men. The Greek classics, by such poets as Homer, are tales written about the deeds and misdeeds of these immortal beings, with their fictitious domicile located on Mt. Olympus.

Out of these imaginings came stories of mythological exploits that account for the gods and goddesses of Greek and Roman mythology, as well as of Hinduism and certain aspects found in Mormonism and other false world religions. The names of their deities have mutated slightly because of the

* 2 Samuel 21:16, 18

language confusion at the Tower of Babel, with names such as Isis, Artemis, Astarte, Aphrodite, Asheroth, Athena, and Diana being given to the goddesses, as well as the variety of names given to their sons and cohorts, including the various Baals, and one in particular named Tammuz.

In the Book of Ezekiel, a fertility god named Tammuz is mentioned. It is in the Book of Ezekiel that the presence of the Lord departs from the temple in Jerusalem because of the idolatrous worship of the goddesses and false gods by the Jewish people.

> So He brought me to the door of the north gate of the LORD's house; and to my dismay, women were sitting there weeping for Tammuz.
>
> —EZEKIEL 8:14

The New Testament tells us that God chained the angelic beings who conjoined with Earth's women in fathering the giants in darkness under the earth. These fallen angels are referred to as the angels "who left their first estate." There is no indication that all of the fallen angels joined in this rebellion, but those that did remain God's prisoners and even today are being held in darkness under the earth awaiting Judgment Day.* At that time they will, no doubt, receive harsh judgment for starting the false goddess mystery religions—a satanic plan that spread worldwide, confusing and leading multitudes away from the true God and condemning millions to an eternal destination in the lake of fire.

---

* Jude 5–7

> And the angels who did not keep their proper domain, but left their own abode, He has reserved in everlasting chains under darkness for the judgment of the great day.
>
> —Jude 6–7

> God did not spare the angels who sinned, but cast them down to hell and delivered them into chains of darkness, to be reserved for judgment.
>
> —2 Peter 2:4–6

The Bible warns against angelic beings who come as angels of light but are really wolves in sheep's clothing. At least two counterfeit religions have been started in recent centuries by angels. One example is the Latter-Day Saints (Mormon) Church. They believe the angel Moroni visited Joseph Smith in a cave and gave him instructions on how to start the Mormon religion, which has some tenets that are shockingly similar to Freemasonry. Another religion started by angels is the religion of Islam.

Seven centuries after the beginning of Christianity, an angelic being had many meetings with Mohammed, giving him instructions on how to start Islam and worship a god called Allah—a god also mentioned in the upper levels of Freemasonry. The New Testament states that those who start false religions—whether man or angel—are accursed.

> But even if we, or an angel from heaven, preach any other gospel to you than what we have preached to you, let him be accursed.*
>
> —GALATIANS 1:8

If we did not know the true origins of the Noah story and if we could not see that there really are mythological gods and goddesses in religions such as Hinduism and the mystery religions, our Western mindset would likely just dismiss all this as silliness. But—though strange—these are the events that can be traced back to the origins of false religions currently in the world today. Even the Muslims fight one group against the other because one group is monotheistic, while the other, in addition to Allah, incorporates a type of goddess in the form of Mohammed's niece in their worship.**

So the Flood in the days of Noah, along with the earlier giants that were conceived through the parentage of angels and human women, were combined in a mythological fantasy world. From it would emerge and evolve the goddess and mystery religions of Greece, Rome, Asia, and beyond. Baptismal regeneration, as a result of the misinterpretation of the Noah and the ark story, would be the basis of the heathen's hope for entry into paradise after their demise.

A respected book to consult regarding their intrusion into Christianity through the Noahic myth is *The Two Babylons* by the Reverend Alexander Hislop. His research authenticates much of the history of the god/goddess beliefs that are known

---

* Galatians 1:8

** Norman Anderson, *Christianity and World Religions* (Leicester, England: Inter-Varsity Press, 1984), 65.

collectively as the mystery religions and is foundational to much of the following information.

Hislop says that in India, the land of a million gods, the main god is known by the name Vishnu, meaning "the preserver." Vishnu's story is similar to Noah's in that he is credited with being supernaturally preserved along with a single righteous family when a great worldwide flood occurred, drowning the rest of the world. In Sanscrit, *Vishnu* means "Noah." In Chaldean, the word for "Noah" is similar: *Ish-nuh* means "Man of rest."*

The Adamic race spread worldwide after their failed attempt to build the Tower of Babel.** God had dispersed the people by diving their single language into various differing languages so that the larger group would not be able to communicate and "do all they had imagined to do."*** The names of the deities originally found at the Tower of Babel also would mutate slightly as they spread out across many lands,**** yet goddess worship had been established and would remain shockingly similar.*****

The names of the original priest and priestess at the pagan tower of Babel were Nimrod and Semiramis. According to books on ancient Greek and Roman religions found in

---

* Ibid., 59. See also Johan Wilson's *India Three Thousand Years Ago.*

** Genesis 11:1–10

*** Genesis 10–11

**** Richard M. Rives, *Too Long in the Sun* (Charlotte, NC: Parakers Publications, 1997), 51-76; Merrill C. Tenney, *The Zondervan Pictorial Encyclopedia of the Bible, vol. 3* (Grand Rapids, MI: Zondervan, 1975), 334.

***** Yves Bonnefoy, *Greek and Egyptian Mythologies* (Chicago: University of Chicago Press, 1992), 246; Alexander Hislop, *The Two Babylons* (Neptune, NJ: Loizeaux Brothers, 1959), 132; J. G. Davies, *The Early Christian Church* (New York: Holt, Rinehart, and Winston, 1965), 69.

the bookstore of the Minneapolis Museum of Art, when Nimrod died, his widow claimed that a son, fathered after her husband's demise, had been conceived by a sunbeam. This gave Tammuz, the son born to her, god status. In the eyes of these ancient peoples, this gave the mother, Semiramis, the stature of mother of god.*

In these religions, the events in the life of Noah have become entwined in the Babylonian myth of Semiramis, mother of the sunbeam-inspired god named Tammuz. It is a "queen of heaven worship," which is found in religions around the world. Examples are Fortuna and Jupiter, Isis and Horus,** and, of course, it has infiltrated the Roman Catholic Church in the form of the Madonna and Son.***

Christians unwittingly enter into observances with the false gods and goddesses of mythology (names vary because of the language change at the tower of Babel) when they celebrate the birthday of Jesus on December 25. In the pagan world, long before Christianity claimed December 25 as the birthday of God's only begotten Son, that date was celebrated as the birthday of pagan gods, including Tammuz, Ra (the sun god of Egypt), Zeus, and Mithra (the Persian version of Tammuz), and others. When Rome conquered Jerusalem, they hung Jewish patriots on the cross of Mithra as a sacrifice to the sun god on December twenty-fifth.****

---

* Bonnefoy, 246; Hislop, 132; Davies, 69.

** Hislop, 140. See also Pompeii, Vol. ii, 150.

*** C. Peter Wagner, *Conquering the Queen of Heaven* (Colorado Springs, CO: Wagner Institute for Practical Ministry, 1998), 31; Dave Hunt, *A Woman Rides the Beast* (Eugene, OR: Harvest House Publishers, 1994), 439. (See Ezekiel 8:14; Jeremiah 7:18.)

**** Ruud, 61–62.

Other events on the Christian calendar that are intertwined with the goddess religions are that of Easter and Lent. Ever wonder why in Lent we mourn forty days before Jesus' death on the cross? The church's Lenten practices can be traced back to the goddess religions, too, (Ezek. 8:14). The fertility god Tammuz was gored by a wild boar and killed. His lover, the goddess Ishtar, descended into the netherworld, where she discovered his organ missing. Ishtar mourned and searched for forty days until the lost was found and Tammuz was restored. Then the two of them ascended back onto Earth amidst immoral revelry at a festival called Easter (Ishtar).* God was incensed that the Hebrew women also participated in the mourning, calling it an abomination.**

A belief in baptismal regeneration has its root in the goddess religions, also called the mystery religions. It was through taking part in water rites that the Chaldeans believed they would be allowed to enter paradise when they died. (Abraham, the father of our faith, was originally from Ur of Chaldea).*** It was also the Chaldeans who initiated sun worship. Those who desired to become followers of the sun god were required to submit to a violently rigorous baptism.**** If they survived the ordeal, they were promised regeneration and forgiveness of all past sins.*****

The ancestors of today's Scandinavians also believed in baptismal regeneration. Worshipers of the pagan god Odin,

---

* Tenney, 334. Ruud, 65-66.

** Ezekiel 8:14

*** Genesis 12:1–2

**** Bonnefoy, 246; Davies, 69.

***** Hislop. 132. See also Eliase Comment, in 8. Greg. Naz., Orat. 4, Gredorii Nazanzine Opera, 245.

they, like infant baptism churches today, practiced a baptism of infants and believed that "the natural guilt and corruption of new-born children" was washed away in a baptism of infants.*

With a belief in baptismal regeneration already in place, it explains why Scandinavians were such easy targets when their rulers asked them to convert from Odin worship to Roman Catholicism, and then, finally, from Roman Catholicism to Lutheranism after the great Reformation. It was only a stone's throw from the other two religions that they had already been practicing.**

In Mexico, half a world away, the practice of infant baptism, with its corresponding practice of baptismal regeneration, was also taking place. When the explorer Cortéz discovered the Aztecs, he was surprised to find them baptizing babies, too. It was strikingly similar to what was already being performed by Roman Catholic missionaries.*** There, too, the god Odin was being worshiped, as well as the queen of heaven, who was also worshiped among the Chaldeans, Persians, and in the Canaanite religions.****

A Mexican***** myth has Wodan (sometimes called Odin), a grandson to Noah, being saved on a raft when most of humanity perished in a great flood.****** He is presented as

---

* Ibid. See also Paul Henri Mallet on Anglo-Saxon baptism in Northern Antiquities, Vol. 1 (Boston, MA: Adamant Media Corporation, 2002) 335.

** Ibid.

*** Ibid. See also Humboldt's *Mexican Researches, Vol. 1*, 185.

**** Ibid. See also Prescott's *Mexico, Vol. 3*, 339–340.

***** According to the ancient traditions collected by Bishop Francis Nunez de la Vega, as reported in Hislop, 132.

****** H. A. Maxwell Whyte, *The Power of the Blood* (Springdale, PA: Whitaker House, 1973), 32–33.

one who cooperated in the construction of a great building undertaken by men to reach the skies.* Once more, we find ties to the Noah story and the accompanying belief in baptismal regeneration.

Sooner or later someone will think to ask where a belief in baptizing babies comes from if baptismal regeneration through infant baptism is not a biblical principle. The scholar in the Roman and Greek mythological classics will immediately recognize the origins of this Roman Catholic doctrine of Limbo as originally coming from a poem titled *The Aeneid*, which was written by Virgil a Roman poet.**

In *The Aeneid*, the story is told of a man named *Aeneas* who descended into the hot, sulphuric regions of hell and finds the souls of tormented infants. It tells of innocent babes that death had cruelly snatched from their mother's bosom before they could be given the rites of the Church—that is, infant baptism.

> Before the gates the cries of babes new-born, whom fate had from their tender mothers torn, assault his ears.***

The drama goes on to speak of the horror of these "wretched babes" who have been eternally excluded from paradise (called the Elysian Fields) because their parents neglected to submit them to a ritual of infant baptism. Now, so the poem goes,

---

* Ibid.,133. See also Humboldt's *Mexican Researches, Vol. 1*, 320.

** Hislop, 239. See also Virgil, *The Aeneid, Book 6.ll*, 576–578; Dryden's Translation—Original, II, 427–429.

*** Virgil, *The Aeneid, Book 6.ll*, 576–578; Dryden's Translation—Original, II, 427–429.

they are to forever lay in torment alongside those who "prodigally threw their souls away" through suicide.*

This, understandably, put great fear into the soft hearts of grieving parents who worried that if they did not have their newborn baptized immediately, they might be sentencing him or her to an eternity of horror. As a result, they hurried their offspring off to the Roman Church, which, they were taught, had the authority to properly minister the rites of baptism.

But now the Roman Catholic Church has changed its mind. It has done away with the myth about Limbo. According to Pope Benedict XVI, they were getting too many calls in their offices having to do with the eternal destination of aborted babies. According to an article in the *Minneapolis Star Tribune* on December 5, 2005, the Roman Catholic Church issued a report to prepare the hearts of the Church world that a change was coming regarding the doctrine of Limbo.

Then, on January 10, 2006, Pope Benedict XVI called a press conference to do the actual business of taking apart the doctrine of Limbo without starting an outcry. He said that Limbo was no longer going to be a part of the Roman Catholic Church belief system because it had always been "only a hypothesis" anyway.**

The next question then should be, What does happen when a baby dies before he is old enough to decide for himself things of an eternal matter? Believers need not fear; God has it all well in hand.

---

* Virgil, Book 6, 586–589, Dryden's Translation–Original, II, 434–436.

** Kevin Horragan, "The Afterlife: Limbo Rocked," Knight-Ridder News Service, January 10, 2006.

> For the unbelieving husband is sanctified by the wife, and the unbelieving wife is sanctified by the husband; otherwise your children would be unclean, but now they are *holy.*
>
> —1 CORINTHIANS 7:14, EMPHASIS ADDED

It is interesting to note that the above verse states that babies and small children of believers are already holy to God—not in need of exorcism. The word *holy* used in that verse is the same word in Greek (*hagios*)* that is used to refer to the Holy Spirit, who God most certainly considers holy and without fault.

Using the Bible as our criterion, it shows that God sees the babies of believers as pure—in the same way as He sees the Holy Spirit. Of course, the time will come when even believer's children reach a time of accountability and are required to choose for themselves whether or not to serve the Lord. But until that day comes, they will enter heaven because of God's grace, should they die prematurely.

---

* James Strong, *Strong's Exhaustive Concordance of the Bible* (Nashville, TN: Thomas Nelson), s.v. "40 (Greek), hagios" (sacred, pure, morally blameless or religious, consecrated or most holy one, saint), "53 (Greek), hagnos" (clean, i.e. innocent, modest, perfect—chaste, clean, pure), "2282 (Greek), thallo" (to warm, to brood, to foster—cherish).

PART II

REACHING HEAVEN'S GATES

Jesus saith unto him, I am the way, the truth, and the life: no man cometh unto the Father, but by me

—JOHN 14:6

10

HONORING THE BLOOD

EVEN BACK IN THE New Testament days, there were false religious leaders who did not like a baptism that required repentance. John the Baptist had come preaching that one must forsake his or her sin and get right with God. It had been prophesied that one like Elijah would be sent before the coming of the Messiah to prepare the people's hearts.

John was an unlikely forerunner of the Messiah. Even his appearance did not conform to the elegant standards of leadership that were displayed in Jesus' day. He was roughly dressed and spoke even rougher words to the Pharisees as he accused them of being full of sin.

But the laypeople? They liked him. They repented of their sins and rushed down to the shores of the Jordan River to be baptized because John had said that if they were truly repentant, they must make an outward exhibition of their sorrow over their sin—and then they would be forgiven.

Jesus took part, too, even though He had no sins of His own of which He needed to repent. Some say He was modeling it for those who were to later believe in Him; others say that it was in response to what priests were required to do to present themselves clean and fresh to perform ministry in the temple. Still others believe that His baptism was the washing that was necessary in order to prepare the Passover Lamb for sacrifice. The timing was right, but who could say? Perhaps it was all three.

But Jesus noticed that the Pharisees, unlike the laypeople, did not line up on the riverbank to be baptized. They did not want to acknowledge that they were imperfect and needed to take part in a baptism that required repentance. When the Pharisees demanded that Jesus tell them by what authority He had overthrown the money changers in the temple, He took the opportunity to address this issue.* He responded to their questioning by saying, "I will tell you if you will first tell me one thing—the baptism of John—was it of man or of God?"

The Pharisees argued over how to answer His question. "If we say it was of man," they said in private amongst themselves, "the Jews will stone us," for they knew the laypeople believed John was a prophet sent by God to help them get ready for the soon-coming Messiah. "But," they continued their discussion, "if we say John's baptism was of God, Jesus will ask us why we didn't take part." So they told Jesus, "We don't know."

Jesus replied, "Neither will I tell you who gave Me authority to chase the moneychangers out of the temple." But He was grieved with them. He knew that their example by refusing to be baptized in a baptism that required repentance was causing many laypeople to miss their destiny. And, indeed, Scripture

* Matthew 21:23–27

states that these false leaders, too, missed their own destiny when they refused this visitation from God.

Lighting candles does not save, infant baptism does not save, worship of Mary and saying the rosary does not save, and going to church does not bring us salvation. Only faith in Jesus saves, for we "were not redeemed with corruptible things, like gold or silver, but with the precious Blood of Christ, as a lamb without blemish and without spot" (1 Pet. 1:18–19). Shedding His Son's Blood was so costly to God that He could, in good conscience, say of our debt of sin, "It is finished."

In order to have repentance and revival in our churches, we must get back to the truth that it is only through the Blood of Christ that we can be saved. God says if we do not honor His Son, we are not honoring Him.* Is it any wonder that God wants His Son acknowledged, and that He wants the finished work of the Cross acknowledged? We have to accept Jesus' Blood in our church congregations. God will accept nothing less than this to eternally pay the price of redemption for the sins humanity.

It was Jesus' Blood that was shed, and it was Jesus who paid the price of our ransom. Neither sprinkling nor being immersed in water pays the price. Denominations that substitute a baptism of infants as the way of salvation are going to find themselves without an advocate on Judgment Day. No one will get into heaven because they were baptized. They will only get in because of the Blood of Jesus.

Death could not hold Jesus because He was without sin. He had never broken God's commandments. Yet in His death, He

---

* John 5:23

tasted death for all of us. He entered into the bowels of hell. Three days later, God raised Him out of there because sin and hell and death could not legally claim a man without sin.

Jesus made an open spectacle out of Satan and his powers and principalities on that day when God raised Him from the dead.* All of this, including His triumphant resurrection, had been planned before the world began as had Jesus' entry into heaven. There He offered His precious Blood on the altar before God. Proof that God accepted the precious blood Christ offered was His resurrection from the dead. He achieved highest honor with the Maker of the universe and today sits on the right hand of the Father, where He will one day judge you and me.

Jesus' Blood was the only sacrifice acceptable to the Father. Had Christ sinned while He was here on Earth, there would have been nothing else the Father would have accepted to release us from our debt of sin. Thus, it is a very serious thing to make light of the precious Blood of Jesus for, "According to the law almost all things are purged with blood, and without the shedding of blood there is no remission" for sin (Heb. 9:22).

The principle of an innocent life required to make a guilty life pure and holy again runs throughout the Bible. Jesus fulfilled the Law, which said if man sins, he dies. Jesus died, but with no sin. Thus, in the economy of heaven, His innocent life could be substituted for our guilty life.** Jesus poured out His lifeblood to God, and God gives us back our life.

This principle has been falsely applied to the Catholic Church's veneration of saints, but saints are not sinless. Thus,

---

* Colossians 2:15

** Galatians 3:13–14

the blood coursing through their veins was not sinless. God looks away when the newly-dead Catholic offers it as their reason to gain heaven. Over the generations, man has proudly refused to admit that his sin brings death, but God sees it differently.

As a good Father, He planned ahead by putting blood in the veins of animals to be sacrificed on the altar to pay man's debt of sin. It was but a temporary measure, for it had been decreed, "The life of the flesh is in the blood, and I have given it to you upon the altar to make atonement for your souls; for it is the blood that makes atonement for the soul" (Lev. 17:11).

God gave specific instructions in the Bible as to how we are to regard the blood. The blood of a human being is not to be shed by another human being except in certain instances of justice, such as a life for a life (in the case of murder). Even the blood of an animal was not to be eaten or drunk when an animal was killed for food. Instead, it was to be poured out on the ground and covered with dust.

One of the many benefits of the Blood of Christ is that it is the only thing that can cleanse mankind's conscience. Scripture says that every person has sinned and is on his way to hell without the blood covering. The power of Jesus' Blood is so great that He needed to die just once to atone for the sin of humanity, unlike the millions of repeated sacrificial offerings of bulls and goats that took place under the old covenant in the Old Testament.

But even with all the animals offered in the Old Testament, mankind's conscience could not be cleansed, for there was no power in the blood of animals. And yet, God used the temporary sacrifice of animals because He knew that in the fullness of time, Christ would shed His Blood once for all of humanity. One sinless Man could do this because it was by the sin of just one man, that sin entered the human race.

So, it was by the Blood of Jesus that man could be declared not guilty under the old covenant as well as under the new covenant.

> For the law, having a shadow of the good things to come, and not the very image of the things, can never with these same sacrifices, which they offer continually year by year, make those who approach perfect. For then would they not have ceased to be offered? For the worshipers, once purged, would have had no more consciousness of sins. But in those sacrifices there is a reminder of sins every year. For it is not possible that the blood of bulls and goats could take away sins.
>
> —Hebrews 10:1–4

God's plan from the very beginning has been that not only would He demand innocent blood to cover our guilt but He would also supply that innocent blood. This is beyond human understanding. By accepting His own Son's offer to provide the innocent blood sacrifice, God opened the doorway, at great cost to Himself, for us to enter heaven when we place our faith in what His Son did for us on the cross.

Justice had been satisfied—a worthy sacrifice made. A way had been opened.

Adam and Eve Knew the Power of the Blood

The account of Adam and Eve, besides teaching us our beginnings, was meant to demonstrate the necessity of blood for restoration of a right relationship with God. It also shows the worthlessness of man's attempts to dream up his own way to get into heaven. To God, man's frail attempts are like filthy rags. He has a better way, a pure and holy way.

God has decreed that He will only accept the shedding of innocent blood to cover the sin of the guilty. In doing so, He planned ahead. On the day of creation, He put the life of the creature in the blood of both humans and animals. That way, the blood would be there later when it would be needed to provide atonement after Adam and Eve sinned in the Garden of Eden.

That is how we know that Adam's fall in the garden did not take God by surprise. Adam and Eve were the first to sin and the first to try to become righteous by some method other than the blood. They had never experienced anything like guilt before, so they decided the awful feelings they were experiencing because of their sin (never having experienced guilt before) were because their bodies were exposed. Their plan was to sew together fig leaves. What have we tried?

Their attempt to supply their own covering failed. God refused to accept it. But in His mercy and compassion, God supplied a covering for them Himself. He shed the blood of an innocent animal and made a covering for them, because without the shedding of blood, there is no remission (forgiveness) of sin. "Also for Adam and his wife the Lord God make tunics of skin, and clothed them" (Gen. 3:21).

While Adam and Eve submitted to God and accepted His blood covering for their sin, their son, Cain, did not. Thus, he was the first person to rebel against the shedding of blood to cover sin, though there have been multitudes since.

The story of Cain and Abel as told in the Genesis 4 account in the Old Testament is not the simple story of brotherly jealousy, the older toward the younger. Far from it! It is the story of Cain's rebellion against God and Abel's willing obedience to His demands. The hostility that arose in Cain against Abel is a symbol of the type of hostility that even today rises in the heart of the unrighteous toward the righteous.

Both Cain and Abel had obviously been taught that a blood sacrifice was what was needed to cover the sin in one's life, because the life is in the blood. Abel, Adam and Eve's second son, understood and honored the value God placed on the blood, even though it was temporary, until Christ came.

Although people would not kill animals for food until after the Flood, it is possible that Abel both chose to raise a garden and maintain a flock of sheep so that he had animals available for sacrifice. In contrast, Cain was a tiller of the land. He rebelliously chose to bring the convenient grains and vegetables he had in his garden as a sacrifice to God instead of the required blood offering.*

This same stubbornness is at the root of all who refuse to symbolically offer to God Christ's blood, shed for them at

* Genesis 4:5–6

Calvary. This is a strange phenomenon, for they are willing to do or bring any number of other strange things as an offering. But complete forgiveness requires the sin-free Blood of Jesus.

False religions today follow the pattern of Cain. They refuse to accept the fact that it is only through the shed Blood of Jesus Christ that they can be made righteous before God. They try many other religious formulas to get to heaven, just as Cain tried to be forgiven by bringing vegetables instead of the blood of a lamb. People have been following in Cain's footsteps ever since. What they offer differs, but the origin of their rebellion is the same.

People were playing this same game back when they gathered together to build the Tower of Babel. They were putting together a false religion because they wanted to find a different way to heaven than the righteousness decreed by the Creator of the universe. They tried charting planets and watching the alignment of the stars, seeking for a one-world order that excluded God.

All false religions devise their own rituals and rules to try to get into the kingdom of heaven. The only thing they will not offer before God is their faith in the shed Blood of His Son, Jesus Christ. But the Blood of His Son was so costly to God that He can only, in good conscience, say, "It will be My way or no way."

Cain's religion says we can be saved by offering vegetables or we can be saved by baptism or we can be saved by going to church or we can be saved by wearing fig leaves or saying the rosary or going to mass. But we will never get into heaven that way. For there is only one God and He has decreed that "without the shedding of blood, there will be no remission [of sin]." We will do well to heed His voice.

Noah Knew the Power of the Blood

As soon as Noah set foot on dry land after the great Flood, the first thing he did was build an altar. There he offered certain clean animals on it as a sacrifice of blood before God. Although offering more than one animal at this important time before multiplication of the species began might have seemed overly extravagant to some because there were so few animals left with which to repopulate the earth.

But that was just what Noah wanted. He wanted to honor God with an expensive and precious sacrifice. God appreciated Noah's sacrifice and blessed him, saying there would always be seedtime and harvest time. He put a rainbow in the sky as a sign of His promise. He said He would never again flood the whole earth.

Abraham Knew the Power of the Blood

When God tested Abraham's faithfulness by demanding that he sacrifice his beloved son, Isaac, Abraham marched up the side of the mountain, bringing with him a blood sacrifice—in this case, his only son.*

But Abraham did not need to kill his only son. When he had proved his love for God was genuine, God did not demand his son, Isaac. Instead, God Himself provided a ram

* Genesis 22

for Abraham's sacrificial offering. Abraham's faith in God was so strong that he believed if God really required the death of Isaac, when he had done the deed, God would restore Isaac back to life.

After all, God had promised Abraham that it was through this son, Isaac, that he would have multitudes of descendants—something that could not happen if Isaac were dead. So Abraham knew God would bring Isaac back to life again, even if he sacrificed him on the altar in order to keep His promise. Abraham is commended because of his great faith, and today he is the father of our faith—both to the Jew and to the Christian.

But unlike Abraham's reprieve with his son, the day would come when there would be no midnight-hour rescue of God's only Son. When His Son hung on the cross, no one intervened on His behalf. Only after God went through with the sacrifice of His Son and offered Him up unto pain and death on the cross was He finally brought back to life, where He now sits in heaven at the right hand of His Father.

The Israelites Knew the Power of the Blood

The story of the children of Israel is not just a story of God setting the captives free. Oh, He does that, of course. He sets the Hebrew slaves free, but even more than that, it is the story of a very uneven power struggle taking place in the heavenlies between Jehovah God and the idolatry of Egypt, with its sun worship and the gods and goddesses of the mystery religions.

At the time of God's aggressive confrontation with the false gods of Egypt, nine terrible plagues had already devastated the nation. God demanded that Pharaoh release His people so they could go into the desert to worship Him. When Pharaoh refused, God gave nine warnings before He applied the power of the blood in the form of the Passover lamb (symbolically a type of the Blood of Christ).

Not one of the false gods that Egypt served was of any help during all the plagues, specifically designed to show the helplessness of lifeless carvings of idols. Finally, Pharaoh had to admit he was powerless against the true God. His gods were useless. He knuckled under, even begging Moses to leave with the Israelites and to go into the desert to worship their God.

Never had the Egyptians seen such a raw display of power as was turned against them in those weeks. God had been patient with their cruelty for four hundred years. Before that time, Pharaoh refused to acknowledge Jehovah as God. As the pharaoh of Egypt, wasn't he himself considered a god? Shouldn't he be worshiped? Besides, what about the other gods of Egypt that Pharaoh served—shouldn't they be worshiped instead of the God of Moses? No, indeed, Pharaoh did not intend to have any part in letting his slaves acknowledge a different God.

After nine warnings (the plagues), God had had enough. He said to Moses and his brother, Aaron the high priest:

> Speak to all the congregation of Israel, saying: "On the tenth of this month every man shall take for himself a lamb, according to the house of his father, a lamb for a household."
>
> —Exodus 12:3

Thus, we know that the Israelites, too, had an understanding of the necessity of the shedding of blood. Before they left Egypt, God taught them the power of the blood by having Moses instigate the Passover Feast. On the night of the feast, each family was to take, kill, and eat a lamb. They were to put the blood of this lamb over their doorpost. Then they were to stay inside the house until morning. God protected all who put themselves under the blood covering—whether Jew or Gentile. They were to be kept safe when the angel of death passed over the land.

The blood of the Passover lambs was a type of the Blood of Christ. The Israelites needed to be obedient to the instructions God gave their leader, Moses. Had they not applied the blood to their doorposts that night, their firstborn, too, would have been slain, as happened to their Egyptian neighbors. It was not their ethnicity that saved them; it was their faith in following God's directions to put the blood over their door.

> And they shall take some of the blood and put it on the two doorpost and on the lintel of the houses where they eat it....For I will pass through the land of Egypt on that night, and will strike all the firstborn in the land of Egypt, both man and beast; and against all the gods of Egypt I will execute judgment: I am the LORD. Now the blood shall be a sign for you on the houses where you are. And when I see the blood, I will pass over you; and the plague shall not be on you to destroy you when I strike the land of Egypt.
>
> —EXODUS 12:7, 12–13

They were to take:

> ...a bunch of hyssop, dip it in the blood that is in the basin, and strike the lintel and the two doorposts with the blood that is in the basin. And none of you shall go out of the door of his house until morning. For the LORD will pass through to strike the Egyptians; and when He sees the blood on the lintel and on the two doorposts, the LORD will pass over the door and not allow the destroyer to come into your houses to strike you.
>
> —EXODUS 12:22–23

According to, Josephus, historian of that day, ten persons were the least number and twenty the most who could partake of one Passover lamb.* Only the highest quality animals were accepted by the Levites for these occasions. No "seconds" were good enough. It is estimated that there were approximately two and a half million Israelites at the time of the first Passover. By doing the math, we see that more than 160,000 lambs were slain on that night alone.

It is impossible to calculate the amount of bloodshed as temporary sacrifices were made during the time period that the old covenant was in effect. Just during the time of King Solomon, for example, when the population increased to five or six million, the slaughter of Passover lambs would have been 400,000 each year. Add to that the daily and evening sacrifices during those years, the double burnt offering on the Sabbath, and the burnt offerings on the great festivals or

* Whyte, *The Power of the Blood.*

special Sabbaths, and you will have some idea how precious is the Blood of the Lamb of God.

God did not choose to use just one lamb to symbolize His Son, the Lamb of God, who would one day take away the sins of the world. He chose to use such a great quantity that the amount cannot even be computed. Even when King Solomon dedicated the Temple on Mount Moriah, the number of animals slaughtered was so great they could not even be counted.* In just one day, he made a peace offering on behalf of the nation of Israel that consisted of the blood of 22,000 oxen and 120,000 sheep.

Things have not changed even today. God still requires the shedding of blood to cover sins. The difference is that He no longer accepts the blood of bulls and goats because His Son has paid the price. Today, the Blood of Christ is the one thing God recognizes as a covering for sin. He is so adamant about this that if we try to substitute something else to provide salvation, like a baptism of infants, He removes His covering over us.

Hence, when the Judaizers were trying to substitute the ritual of circumcision in place of complete faith in Christ's blood, God drew back and said they would fall from grace if they did that: "Indeed I, Paul, say to you that if you become circumcised, Christ will profit you nothing. And I testify again to every man who becomes circumcised that he is a debtor to keep the whole law. You have become estranged from Christ, you who attempt to be justified by law; you have fallen from grace."**

The Old Testament door to salvation is closed forever. Christ has been crucified. The New Testament door is open.

---

* 1 Kings 8:5; 2 Chronicles 5:6

** Galatians 5:2–4

It has been ratified by Christ's shed blood. The Father God recognizes no other way into His presence than by the shed blood of His Son. Jesus said, "I am the way, the truth, and the life. No one comes to the Father except through Me" (John 14:6). Anyone who tries to get into heaven by using fig leaves to cover his front insults God and is ignored.

Although the special blood that was in Jesus' body carried no sin, Jesus allowed Himself to be sentenced to die a criminal's death. He knew His sinless blood would be acceptable to the Father as a covering for mankind's sin. Because Adam, as one man, had brought sin into the world, Jesus, as one Man, could bring the cure.*

He could "pick up the check" for our sin because He did not have any sin of His own for which He needed to pay a penalty. So, He hung on the cross and mankind's sin entered into Him. He died and descended into hell for three days, paying the penalty for our sin. That is why the penalty for our sin is already written off, whether we choose to take Him up on it or not.

Each individual makes his own choice whether to repent and make Jesus Lord or not. The Bible says, "That if you confess with your mouth the Lord Jesus and believe in your heart that God has raised Him from the dead, you will be saved" (Rom. 10:9).

Meanwhile the Blood Jesus shed for mankind was still untainted by sin, for He had never engaged in sin of any kind. And when God raised Him from the dead after three days, mankind's all-time sin debt was fully paid. Now the only

---

* 1 Corinthians 15:22

thing man may be convicted of at the Judgment Seat is not believing in Jesus, who God sent.*

Jesus, for His part, was able to say victoriously, "I am the resurrection and the life. He who believes in Me, though he may die, he shall live" (John 11:25). He had tasted death for all of us.** He had given the perfect life, which was in His perfect Blood. He had been as a slaughtered lamb on the Passover altar, an act done intentionally and purposefully, a perfect life for our guilty life. He set us free from the penalty of eternal death.

Never underestimate the power of the Blood of Jesus. "For the life of the flesh is in the blood, and I have given it to you upon the altar to make an atonement for your souls; for it is the blood that makes atonement for the soul" (Lev. 17:11). And, "Without shedding of blood there is no remission" of sin (Heb. 9:22).

There is redemption only in the shed Blood of that spotless Lamb of God, Jesus Christ. God Himself, as sovereign ruler of the universe, can choose to use what He wants to provide salvation and forgiveness of sin. He has chosen His own Son to die as a Passover Lamb to take away the sin of the world. And, without His Son's Blood as our covering [or "wedding garment," as it is called in the following Scripture passage], no man will be accepted at the heavenly wedding supper of His Son.

There have been more than three hundred prophecies made over the centuries by many different prophets. All are recorded in the Old Testament. They point to Jesus Christ and the fact that the Messiah is returning a second time to set up

---

* John 3:18

** Hebrews 2:9

His kingdom here on Earth. He is coming for a bride made up of worldwide believers who have accepted His Blood sacrifice as their way of atonement. That means they have been washed by the Blood Jesus shed on Calvary.

The number has been growing over the centuries of men and women, boys and girls made righteous and set free by the Blood of the Lamb. It will be a joyous day for those who have put on the wedding garment of the shed Blood of the Lamb. Will you be there? Jesus told several parables to help understand this concept, one of which is printed below.

In the following story, as you read, you will note that the king represents God; the king's son, who is about to be married, represents Jesus; the original invited wedding guests who did not bother to come are the Jews; and, last but not least, are we, the Gentiles and derelicts who were invited to come when the Jews failed to come.

But note, also, that when one of the Gentile heathen wandered into the wedding without having on the proper clothing, he was cast out of the wedding supper and into outer darkness where there will be weeping and gnashing of teeth.

This suggests that the arrogant would-be guest knew that he needed a proper covering to attend the gala affair but had refused to accept what the king had supplied for the wedding guests. He had tried to get in by doing things his own way, however, the groom's father had turned him away, and he was sent to an awful place.

He was not allowed to take part in the feast prepared for those who were wearing the proper garments—that is, those who had accepted the Blood of Christ, the only garment God recognizes and accepts.

And Jesus answered and spoke to them again by parables and said: "The kingdom of heaven is like a certain king who arranged a marriage for his son, and sent out his servants to call those who were invited to the wedding; and they were not willing to come. Again, he sent out other servants, saying, "Tell those who are invited, 'See, I have prepared my dinner; my oxen and fatted cattle are killed, and all things are ready. Come to the wedding." But they made light of it and went their ways, one to his own farm, another to his business. And the rest seized his servants, treated them spitefully, and killed them. But when the king heard about it, he was furious. And he sent out his armies, destroyed those murderers, and burned up their city. Then he said to his servants, 'The wedding is ready, but those who were invited were not worthy. Therefore go into the highways, and as many as you find, invite to the wedding.' So those servants went out into the highways and gathered together all whom they found, both bad and good. And the wedding hall was filled with guests. "But when the king came in to see the guests, he saw a man there who did not have on a wedding garment. So he said to him, 'Friend, how did you come in here without a wedding garment?' And he was speechless. Then the king said to his servants, 'Bind him hand and foot, take him away, and cast him into outer darkness; there will be

> weeping and gnashing of teeth. For many are called, but few are chosen."
>
> —Matthew 22:1–14

It is important to note that in order to be present at the wedding supper, which symbolizes heaven, the king required a covering in the form of a proper wedding garment. The Blood of God's Son provided that wedding garment. Our faith (belief) makes it ours:

> Just as man is destined to die once, and after that to face judgment, so Christ was sacrificed once to take away the sins of many people; and he will appear a second time, not to bear sin, but to bring salvation to those who are waiting for him.
>
> —Hebrews 9:27–28, niv

The price has been paid; the choice is ours.

> He himself bore our sins in his body on the tree, so that we might die to sins and live for righteousness; by his wounds you have been healed. For you were like sheep going astray, but now you have returned to the Shepherd and Overseer of your souls.
>
> —Hebrews 10:24–25, niv

11

Why Does the Church Rage Against Biblical Water Baptism?

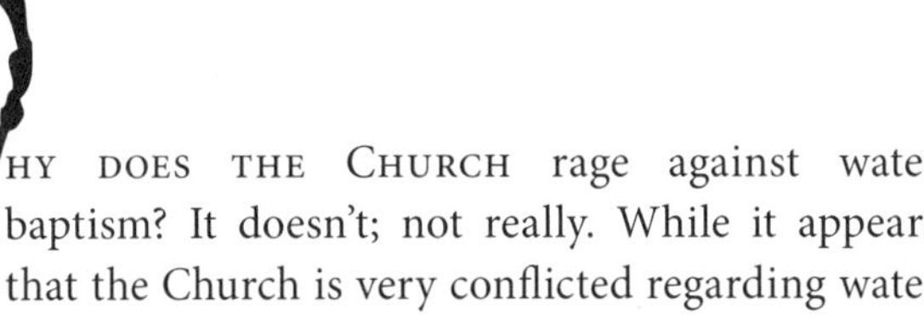

Why does the Church rage against water baptism? It doesn't; not really. While it appears that the Church is very conflicted regarding water baptism—indeed, one branch practices a baptism of infants and the other a baptism that symbolizes what happens to believers when they put their trust in Jesus Christ—it is Satan who rages against water baptism.

This is because water baptism, in its biblical form, is teamed up with receiving the Holy Spirit. There are few Christians who are not familiar with what happened when Jesus, their Lord and Savior, was baptized in water: He received the infilling of the Holy Spirit, who provided all the power that was supplied in Jesus' ministry while here on Earth. Certainly the devil does not want that to happen in the lives of the millions of Christians who are being born into the kingdom of God.

It was prophesied in Scripture that Satan would try to destroy the full plan, which included biblical water baptism. We know the real reason was to stop the church's empowerment by substituting a false water baptism after Jesus (the Man

Child) was resurrected into heaven and the dragon (Satan) took off after the woman (God's people):

> So the serpent [Satan] spewed water out of his mouth like a flood after the woman [the Church], that he might cause her to be carried away by the flood.
>
> —Revelations 12:15

Times have not changed. The adversary of our souls still desires to wipe out biblical water baptism so that believers will not receive the gift of the Holy Spirit and be empowered—as was Jesus—to live a successful Christian life. Mankind is at fault, too. Scripture says, "…you do always resist the Holy Spirit, as your fathers did, so do you. (See Acts 7:51.)

There is a second reason why Satan wanted to substitute a false water baptism for biblical water baptism and the baptism of the Holy Spirit. If he could get rid of God's Holy Spirit, could he then stand a chance of averting God's curse put on him back in the Garden of Eden?

> [God said] He [the Seed of the woman] shall bruise your head, And you shall bruise His [Jesus'] heel."
>
> —Genesis 3:15

So it all goes back to the garden. Satan's obsession has been to defeat God's plan any way he can. He has used mankind as his unwitting vessel. God's perfect plan (and the one that is triumphing) was that His Holy Spirit would empower people who have chosen to be part of His kingdom of light. Empowered by the Holy Spirit, they, in turn, would pull down the works of darkness that Satan has put in place to keep mankind from discovering the way to heaven.

I naively thought the most important role in this eternal drama would be the part Martin Luther played in restoring the Church at the time of the great Reformation of the 1500s. But as my research progressed, I have had to accept the fact that Luther is just a bit player in the greatest drama of all time—that of restoring mankind to favor with God.

Luther, along with a host of others, failed to complete his God-given assignment and lost the opportunity to restore the Church to its New Testament purity. Instead, he was deceived into drawing back into the old Church, which also carries the goddess religion influence of baptismal regeneration through a baptism of infants.

So the drama continues. The end draws near. The greatest drama ever conceived is playing out across the world's stage today. It is the greatest love story ever told. Its protagonist is the most magnificent, magnanimous, and merciful—but its antagonist is the cruelest.

Act 1 is about God

He is Jehovah, and the same yesterday, today, and forever. He is all-powerful and all-loving, but He is also holy and pure and will not tolerate evil. He is Jehovah-Shammah—the Lord who is there; Jehovah-Shalom—the Lord who is our peace; Jehovah-Ra-ah—the Lord who is our Shepherd; Jehovah-Jireh—the Lord who will provide for us; Jehovah-Nissi—the Lord who is our banner, our captain, our victor; Jehovah-Tsidkenu—the Lord who is our righteousness; and

Jehovah-Rapha—the Lord who heals us.* And He cares about us, His creation.

Satan, up to the point of his fall from heaven, had been God's top-of-the-line, deluxe model; the leader of worship; and the most beautiful of all His creatures. Then, through rebellion against God, he fell. Now he is reduced to eventual judgment in the lake of fire. Meanwhile, God has made mankind to take his position. Satan hates God, and he hates the people He has made.

God loved His creation. Every afternoon, in the cool of the day, He would come down into the garden to visit with Adam and Eve.

Satan's jealousy knew no bounds. He was determined to defile Adam and Eve so that he could spoil God's enjoyment of them and take over their God-given place of dominion in the earth. He wanted to spoil Adam because he had learned the hard way that a holy God could not fellowship with a fallen Adam, so he planned to spoil God's enjoyment of Adam and Eve. He knew God cannot commune with that which is impure and unholy. If He tried, the fire of His holiness would consume them, so God had to back away from man—for a time.

You and I are still in the fiery furnace down here. Each person has a specified, individual time to walk on planet Earth. Satan needs to break down that person's trust in God so that he can keep him blinded to the truth until his time on Earth is over so that he refuses God's offer of rescue.

God looked for a man who, because of his trust in Him,

---

* F. F. Bosworth, *Christ the Healer*, 32.

could be singled out to become the "father" of a righteous race. Through this race, He would send a Redeemer.

God might have used Adam, but Adam's unrighteous son killed his righteous son. So, Adam's grandchildren were not raised up in godliness.

God made a covenant with Noah, but Noah's children were not all trained up in the ways of God. His unrighteous son and their descendants rebelled against God at the Tower of Babel and started the goddess religions.

Abraham, because of his faith in God, became that person for which God was looking. One of his sons was willing to be raised up in godliness. Abraham would eventually become the father of two different streams of people: the descendants of Isaac and the descendants of Ishmael.

Isaac was trained up in the ways of God and became the forefather of both Judaism and, later, Christianity. Ishmael would start a different religion, one patched together out of paganism and snatches of Old and New Testament fabric. As with all syncretisms, it bypassed Jehovah who will only accept pure worship.

But in Abraham, God had what He wanted after waiting centuries. He would claim as His own the descendants of Abraham; the Jews, biological sons and daughters of Abraham; and the Christians, who came one by one out from all the nations of the world.

Meanwhile, until the once-for-all, actual, physical coming of His Son Jesus, blood sacrifices would be necessary to cover the guiltiness of God's people. God cut covenant with them. Through the shedding of animal blood, always necessary in a covenant, the Israelites of the Old Testament built a relationship with God.

Act 2 is about Jesus

Jesus is God Jehovah and the Son of God. He is the Alpha and the Omega, the beginning and the end. He, of His own free will, chose to come down to Earth to take the punishment that would otherwise be dealt us after our physical death.

God made man an eternal spirit. Because man's spirit was corrupted in the Fall, a renewed spirit, in which God houses His own Holy Spirit, is necessary if we are to live together harmoniously with God now and throughout eternity.

The unrenewed spirit of man cannot enter heaven. It has an increasing bend toward evil, which must be contained in the lake of fire. The man who dies unrepentant does not have the renewed spirit (converted heart) that comes with repentance. For this reason, the unrepentant soul must enter the lake of fire so that his tendency toward evil is contained by the lake of fire.

This is necessary because his spirit, and the power inherent in it, will never die. It would continue to bring corruption, which is unacceptable in heaven.

God has a plan so that man can receive the renewed spirit he needs to enter heaven. It is by repentance and faith that we become new creations. Old things pass away.

> Therefore, if anyone is in Christ, he is a new creation; old things have passed away; behold, all things have become new.
>
> —2 Corinthians 5:17

In summary, at Jesus' sacrificial death on the cross at Calvary, a new and better covenant was ratified. The new covenant is a continuation of God's mighty plan laid out in the old covenant. This plan included making atonement for the sinfulness of man. The death of God's only Son would be necessary to cleanse mankind and provide a ransom to rescue fallen Adam out of Satan's clutches.

Jesus volunteered for this position. The shed blood of that one innocent Man/God, Jesus Christ, paid the price for each guilty member of Adam's fallen race. At the time of creation, God knew man would fall, but He wanted sons and daughters. And so, He made a provision ahead of time. He put blood in man's body and in the bodies of the other creatures He made. This provided the vehicle of blood in a living creature so that atonement could be made. It was such a simple plan but so profound.

So when someone asks you, "All religions are alike. What's so different about Christianity? How is it any different than all the other religions?" All of God's children can say, "The Blood of Christ makes it different."

They can say, "No other religion claims to have a God who sent His Son to die for them." And we can say, "Only Christianity has a God who cares enough about people that He shed His own Son's blood so that man might be set free to reap eternal life."

Then tell them that no other religion has a God who can be proven historically to have existed and to have walked this planet Earth. Tell them no other religion can claim to have a God who is so interested in the day-to-day life of His people that He wrote a book that would give them gracious instructions on how to navigate this life safely.

Tell them God can do this because it was by one man, Adam, that sin entered the human race, so by one Man, Jesus Christ, atonement for that sin can be made. We know that His holy blood was accepted—and would become a ransom price for us—because God put His stamp of approval on the blood Christ shed when He raised Him from the dead. Nor was this done in a corner. Five hundred were witnesses when the resurrected Christ ascended back into heaven. Even in secular history books, it is acknowledged that Jesus Christ was a real person who lived and died here on planet Earth.

Remind again those who want to know that no other god (or goddess) has given their followers a book that has over three hundred prophecies in it that have proven His authenticity. Taking into account only twenty-one of these prophecies that needed to come to pass in the twenty-four-hour period surrounding His crucifixion, there is only a 1 in 537,000,000 chance of this coming to pass without Him being who He says He is. Now do the math for three hundred prophecies that have come to pass. It is no wonder that many believe that a Messiah who came as promised the first time will again come as promised the second time.

The world is now one prophecy away from the fulfillment of every single one necessary before the second coming of Jesus. The statistical probability of that happening accidentally is almost nothing.

Who else can say such a thing about their god? This God is calling out to you. He has purposely made salvation easy.

Only two things are now necessary. Scripture tells us what they are.

> If you confess with your mouth the Lord Jesus and believe in your heart that God has raised Him from the dead, you will be saved. For with the heart one believes unto righteousness, and with the mouth confession is made unto salvation.
>
> —Romans 10:9–10

Won't you call out to God now? He says He will be found by all those who seek Him with all their heart.

12

What the Bible Says About Salvation

Christ, as the Redeemer, is coming for His Church. Jesus said:

> I am the way, the truth, and the life. No one comes to the Father except through Me.
>
> —John 14:6

> All that the Father gives Me will come to Me, and the one who comes to Me I will by no means cast out.
>
> —John 6:37

> For all have sinned and fall short of the glory of God, being justified freely by His grace through the redemption that is in Christ Jesus, whom God set forth as a propitiation by His blood, though faith, to demonstrate His righteousness, because in His forbearance God had passed over the sins that were previously committed, to demonstrate at the present time His righteousness, that He might

> be just and the justifier of the one who has faith in Jesus.
>
> —ROMANS 3:23–26

> If you confess with your mouth the Lord Jesus and believe in your heart that God has raised Him from the dead, you will be saved. For with the heart one believes unto righteousness, and with the mouth confession is made unto salvation...Whoever believes on Him will not be put to shame....For "whoever calls upon the name of the LORD shall be saved."
>
> —ROMANS 10:9–11, 13

God made it simple for us because He is not willing that any should perish.* If you want eternal life and believe that Jesus is God's Son and that He died, was buried, and resurrected, tell Him. Pray your own prayer, or say something like this:

> *God, I believe that Jesus is Your only begotten Son and that He died, was buried, and that He rose again. I choose to make Jesus the Lord of my life. Come into my heart, Lord Jesus. Amen.*

Now, be baptized in water! Make Jesus truly Lord of your life. The Bible says He commanded us to be baptized in His name after we believe. It doesn't matter if you have already been baptized as a baby. Infant baptism is not found in the Bible, so it does not count.

---

* 2 Peter 3:9

We are to be rebaptized if we have been baptized into something other than Jesus' name. Rebaptism is not a problem for God. In the early Church, rebaptism was dealt with as a very unimportant issue as long as the new disciples received the official Bible baptism of believers, that of the baptism into the name of Jesus.

> And it happened, while Apollos was at Corinth, that Paul, having passed through the upper regions, came to Ephesus. And finding some disciples he said to them, "Did you receive the Holy Spirit when you believed?" So they said to him, "We have not so much as heard whether there is a Holy Spirit." And he said to them, "Into what then were you baptized?" So they said, "Into John's baptism." Then Paul said, "John indeed baptized with a baptism of repentance, saying to the people that they should believe on Him who would come after him, that is, on Christ Jesus." When they heard this, they were baptized in the name of the Lord Jesus.
>
> —Acts 19:1–5

Then tell your priest or pastor that you want to take part in biblical—full-immersion—water baptism. This is for every believer. It is the way of the Cross.

God's provision for us was never to change until the second coming of Christ and includes receiving the gift of the Holy Spirit. In all the examples given in the Book of Acts after the Day of Pentecost, if the Holy Spirit was not openly manifested, before or after water baptism, disciples were dispatched to lay hands on them and bring them into that experience. Neither water baptism nor receiving the Holy Spirit was taken casually.*

If your pastor or priest won't baptize you or rebaptize you after you believe, God will help you find one that will, for this is the full program of God. Baptism doesn't save you, but it shows God that your faith is genuine.

> Repent, and let every one of you be baptized in the name of Jesus Christ for the remission of sins; and you shall receive the gift of the Holy Spirit. For the promise is to you and to your children, and to all who are afar off, as many as the Lord our God will call.
>
> —ACTS 2:38–39

Take stock now. The Bible says that faith without actions is dead.** Jesus commanded baptism.***

---

* Samaritans—Acts 8:1, 17; Ethiopian eunuch—Acts 8:26–38; Saul/Paul's conversion—Acts 9:1–19; Cornelius's household—Acts 10:1–48; Lydia's household—Acts 16:11–15; Philippians jailer's household—Acts 16:25–34; the Ephesians—Acts 19:1–10

** James 2:17

*** Matthew 28:19; Mark 16:16

Appendix A

TEN MYTHS OF INFANT BAPTISM

Myth 1: It is taught by some that babies are saved by infant baptism.

But the Bible does not say that. The following passage is almost always taken out of context. It is not about infant baptism. Jesus was actually responding to His disciples' question about which of them would be greatest in the kingdom of heaven.

> Then Jesus called a little child to Him, set him in the midst of them, and said, "Assuredly, I say to you, unless you are converted and become as little children, you will by no means enter the kingdom of heaven. Therefore whoever humbles himself as this little child is the greatest in the kingdom of heaven.
>
> —Matthew 18:2–4

Myth 2: It is taught by some that the following verse teaches a baptism of infants.

But the Bible does not say that. This verse is often taken out of context to refer to a baptism of infants. Actually, in this verse Jesus instigated a typical Jewish blessing of little children that is often done in certain denominations as a form of dedication to the Lord.

> Then little children were brought to Him that He might put His hands on them and pray, but the disciples rebuked them. But Jesus said, "Let the little children come to Me, and do not forbid them; for of such is the kingdom of heaven." And He laid His hands on them and departed from there.
>
> —Matthew 19:13–15

Myth 3: It is taught by some that circumcision saves.

But the Bible does not say that. It says that circumcision does not save.

> Indeed I, Paul, say to you that if you become circumcised, Christ will profit you nothing....you who attempt to be justified by law [ritual]; you have fallen from grace...For in Christ Jesus neither circumcision nor uncircumcision avails anything, but faith working through love.
>
> —Galatians 5:2, 4, 6

> For we say that faith was accounted to Abraham for righteousness. How then was it accounted? While he was circumcised, or uncircumcised? Not while circumcised, but while uncircumcised.
>
> —Romans 4:9–10

Myth 4: It is taught by some that infant baptism is a type of Old Testament circumcision.

But the Bible does not say that. First, there is no record of infant baptisms in the New Testament church. Second, the Bible does not say that Infant Baptism is a thinly veiled type of circumcision (or any other kind).

Myth 5: It is taught by some that infant baptism is scriptural because all households included infants.

But the Bible does not say that. There are five examples of household baptisms given in the New Testament. In four examples, it is clear that all first believed and then were baptized.

1. The jailer's household (See Acts 16:16–34, esp. v. 34.)
2. Cornelius's household (See Acts 10:1–48, esp. vv. 1, 44.)
3. Stephanas's household (See 1 Corinthians 16:15.)
4. Crispus's household (See Acts 18:8.)

In the fifth example, the Bible does not specifically state that Lydia's whole household believed before they were baptized. On the other hand, it infers that this is true. We know Lydia and her household were devout believers in God. We know that the apostle Paul expounded the gospel to all gathered at the river for their prayer time and that all responded to his preaching by being baptized, so they probably were believers. But, the Bible does not say so in black and white. Thus, infant baptism theology seems to rest on the silence about the faith of Lydia's household, since clearly circumcision cannot be used. The Bible says that circumcision does not save and, in fact, causes one to lose their salvation because they are not putting faith in the shed blood of Jesus Christ alone.

Myth 6: It is taught by some that infant baptism is necessary for babies in case they die prematurely and go into limbo.

But the Bible does not say that. It says that God considers the offspring of believers to be holy. This is the same word *holy*, as used in the Bible for the Holy Spirit. God would not send His Holy Spirit to hell, and believer's babies do not go into hell (or Limbo):

> For the unbelieving husband is sanctified by the wife, and the unbelieving wife is sanctified by the husband; otherwise your children would be *unclean*, but now they are *holy*.
>
> —1 CORINTHIANS 7:14, EMPHASIS ADDED

The infant baptism myth about babies dying and going into Limbo does not come from the Bible. It comes out of the mythology of heathenism. The reader of Greek and Roman classics will recognize Limbo from the Roman drama *The Aeneid*. Written by the well-known author Virgil, it tells of the plight of his character *Aeneas*.

The story tells of Aeneas's visit to the horrific sulfur and flame-filled regions of the netherworld. There Aeneas finds the souls of tormented babies who, having been torn from their mother's breasts in death, must remain in Limbo outside hell's gates without ever having hope of heaven because their parents had not made sure they were given the rites of baptism before they died.

> Before the gates the cries of babes new-born, whom fate had from their tender mothers torn, assault his ears.*

Virgil's character in the play speaks of wretched babes who fate has forever sentenced to spend their eternity next to foolish persons who prematurely threw their life away through suicide. Many false ideas were added to Church doctrines by those who had previously been steeped in Greek mythology and the goddess and mystery religions.

> The next in place and punishment are they who prodigally threw their souls away, fools, who, repining at their wretched state, and loathing anxious life, suborned their fate.**

In other words, out of ancient Roman mythology comes the belief that a baptism of babies is necessary so they don't die and go to hell (go into Limbo). For centuries, the Roman Catholic Church taught a belief in something called Limbo, but on December 5, 2006, the pope called a news conference to let the world know that they had changed their mind. Babies would not now be sent to Limbo if they died unbaptized.

Pope Benedict XVI said that, all along, Limbo had merely been a hypothesis of their church. Because they were getting so many calls from distraught grandparents and mothers

---

* Virgil, *The Aeneid, Book 6.II,* 576–578, Dryden's Translation—Original, II, 427–429.

** Virgil, *The Aeneid, Book 6,* 586-589, Dryden's Translation—Original, II, 434-436.

about what happened to aborted babies, he said they decided to drop Limbo from Catholic beliefs.

Myth 7: It is taught by some theologians that infant baptism joins us to the family of God.

But the Bible doesn't say this. It says that the Holy Spirit does this! Infant baptism is stealing the credit for something done by God's Holy Spirit.

> For by one Spirit, we were all baptized into one body—whether Jews or Greeks, whether slaves or free—and have all been made to drink into one Spirit.
>
> —1 CORINTHIANS 12:13

Myth 8: It is taught by some that the Holy Spirit is given through infant baptism.

But the Bible does not say that. It says that the Holy Spirit is given when we believe, by faith, in what Jesus did for us on the cross. The Bible says we cannot receive the Holy Spirit by a ritual, only by faith:

> O foolish Galatians!...Did you receive the Spirit by the works of the law, or by the hearing of faith? Are you so foolish? Having begun in the Spirit, are you now being made perfect by the flesh?...For as many as are of the works of the law are under the curse; for it is written, "Cursed is everyone who does not continue in all things which are written in the book of the law, to do them." But that no

> one is justified by the law in the sight of God is evident, for "the just shall live by faith."
>
> —GALATIANS 3:1–3, 10–11

Myth 9: It is taught by some that because John the Baptist sovereignly received the Holy Spirit in his mother's womb, the Holy Spirit is imparted to a baby during infant baptism.

But this is not true. The Old Testament is a different dispensation. The Holy Spirit sovereignly came upon prophets, kings, and priests under the old covenant for a specific task. John the Baptist's situation was that he was anointed to be a prophet while still in his mother's womb, and thus the Spirit of God was given to him at that time. The old covenant was in effect at that time because Jesus had not yet shed His Blood, which ratified the new covenant. But under the new covenant, there are no examples given of the Holy Spirit empowering people before they are born.

Myth 10: It is taught by some that the Great Commission teaches that baptism saves.

The Bible does not teach this. It specifically reads that salvation is by faith, for it says that if one does not believe, he will be condemned.

> He who believes and is baptized will be saved; but he who does not believe will be condemned.
>
> —MARK 16:16

It is important to note the word *saved* in this passage does not just mean "going to heaven." It also means deliverance and provision. When the above verse is read with this knowledge, the verse fits neatly into New Testament doctrines.

> Saved (Greek, *sozo*): *Save* means the spiritual and eternal salvation granted to new believers immediately upon their conversion. Included in its meaning is temporal deliverance, material provision, deliverance from danger, etc., in addition to eternal life.*

Thus, a correct understanding of the Mark 16:16 verse which includes the word *saved*, would be as follows: "He who does not believe will be condemned; however, he who both believes and is baptized will receive both future eternal spiritual benefits and temporal benefits and deliverance from bad things while down here on Earth when he becomes a Christian."

---

* *Hebrew-Greek Key Word Study Bible*, 1760.

Author's Page

JUDY MCKENZIE MCCLARY RESIDES in the Twin Cities with her husband of more than forty years. Concerned because the Church is divided into two different streams, has two modes of baptism, and teaches two wildly-different methods for getting to heaven—one believing baptism saves and the other believing it doesn't—McClary began her search for the truth about the infant baptism roots of her mainline denominational church.

While working on a theology degree, McClary had access to libraries and ancient books not usually available to the average layperson and so was able to unravel the mystery of why the Church teaches two such diametrically-opposed ways to get to heaven. A lifelong scholar of the Bible, McClary has studied an ecumenical overview of Church doctrines in her search for the truth. She has taken classes at Maranatha College, Life-Blood School of Ministry, Lutheran Lay Ministry Training Center, Berean College, Living Word Bible Institute, Anoka-Ramsey Community College, and the University of Minnesota.

The author would love to have your testimony of your own personal experience in believer water baptism. Please e-mail them to her for possible inclusion in a future book on people's experience as they obediently took part in the amazing—full immersion—adventure into the baptism in the name of Jesus for believers. E-mail her at: BaptismTestimonies@allaboutbaptism.com

OTHER BOOKS IN THE UNVEILING THE MYSTERIES OF BAPTISM SERIES

SEE AUTHOR'S WEB SITE—WWW.ALLABOUTBAPTISM.COM

Volume 2

Water Baptism: Signing the Contract

Discover the God-given way to authenticate the genuineness of your faith and receive biblical baptism's many benefits at the same time.

Volume 3

Seven Letters to the Infant Baptism Churches: A Layperson Speaks Out

Seven letters written by a layperson and mailed off one by one to her church as the author researched Christian history and compared her church's doctrines to the Bible.

Volume 4, coming in 2009

Goddesses in the Church: What Infant Baptism Has Done to the Christian and the Jew

Watch as the goddess religions prepare to step out of mainline denominational church closets. See what history has to say about the damage done through infant baptism as it splits the church and attacks both Christian and Jew.

Getting to Know the Holy Spirit's Joyful Presence in Your Life

A 12 week Bible study for your discussion group.

www.allaboutbaptism.com

BIBLIOGRAPHY

Alex, Ben. *Martin Luther: The German Monk Who Changed the Church*. Victor Books/SP Publications, Inc., 1995.

Anderson, Sir Norman. *Christianity and World Religions*. Leicester, England: InterVarsity Press, 1984.

Arendzen, J. P. "Gnosticism," *New Advent: The Catholic Encyclopedia*, Vol. 6. New York, 1909. www.newadvent.org.

Armstrong, O. K. and Armstrong M. M. *The Indomitable Baptists*. Garden City, NJ: Doubleday & Company, 1967.

Beale, J. L. *Rise to Newness of Life*. Nappanee, IN: Evangel Press, 1974.

Bettenson, H. S., ed. *Documents of the Christian Church*, 2nd ed. London, England: Oxford University Press, 1963.

Bingham, D. Jeffrey. *Pocket History of the Church*. Downers Grove, IL: InterVarsity Press, 2002.

Booker, R. *The Miracle of the Scarlet Thread*. Shippensburg, PA: Destiny Image Publishers, 1981.

Brant, I. *James Madison: 1787-1800*. Indianapolis, IN: Bobbs-Merrill Company, 1950.

Broadbent, E. H. *The Pilgrim Church*. Grand Rapids, MI: Gospel Folio Press, 1999.

Brim, B. *The Blood and the Glory*. Tulsa, OK: Harrison House, 1995.

Bruce, F. F. *The International Bible Commentary with the NIV*. Grand Rapids, MI: Zondervan Publishing House, 1979.

Bruce. F. F. *The Spreading Flame*. Grand Rapids, MN: Wm. B. Erdmans Publishing, 1995.

The Catechism of the Catholic Church. Mahwah, NJ: Paulist Press, 1994.

Davies, J. G. *The Early Christian Church*. New York: Holt, Rinehart, and Winston, 1965.

DeArteaga, W. *Quenching the Spirit: Examining Centuries of Opposition to the Movement of the Holy Spirit.* Lake Mary, FL: Creation House, 1992.

Dickens, A. G. *The Counter Reformation.* New York: Harcourt, Brace & World, 1969.

Dolan, J. P. *History of the Reformation.* New York: Descleo Company, 1965.

Dyck, C. J., ed. *An Introduction to Mennonite History.* Scottsdale, PA: Herald Press, 1967.

Erikson, E. H. *Young Man Luther: A Study in Psychoanalysis and History.* New York, NY: Norton, 1958.

Foxe, J. *Foxe's Books of Martyrs.* Springdale, PA: Whitaker House, 1981.

Foxe, John, rewritten and updated by Harold J. Chadwick, *Foxe's Book of Martyrs: Updated to the 21st Century.* Gainesville, FL: Bridge-Logos, 2001.

Friedenthal, R. *Luther: His Life and Times.* New York: Harcourt, Brace & Jovanovich, 1970.

Gollian, G. L. *Moravian in Two Worlds.* New York: Columbia University Press, 1967.

Grimm, H. J. *The Reformation Era: 1500-1650.* New York: Macmillan, 1973.

Gundry, R. H. *A Survey of the New Testament,* 3rd ed. Grand Rapids, MI: Zondervan Publishing House, 1994.

Hayford, J. *Hayford's Bible Handbook.* Nashville, TN: Thomas Nelson Publishers, 1995.

Hinn, B. *The Blood.* Orlando, FL: Creation House, 1993.

Hislop, A. *The Two Babylons.* Neptune, NJ: Loizeaux Brothers, 1916.

Horn, W. M. *Growth in Grace.* Philadelphia, PA: Muhlenberg Press, 1951.

Hostetler, J. A. *Hutterite Society.* Baltimore, MD: John Hopkins University Press, 1974.

Hostetler, J. & Huntington, G. *The Hutterites in North America.* New York: Holt, Rinehart, and Winston, 1980.

Huggins, L. *The Blood Speaks.* South Plainfield, NJ: Bridge Publications, 1954.

Hunt, D. *A Woman Rides the Beast.* Eugene, OR: Harvest House Publishers, 1994.

Hurstfield, J. *The Reformation Crisis.* New York: Barnes & Noble, 1965.

Inter-Lutheran Commission on Worship. *The Lutheran Book of Worship.* Minneapolis, MN: Augsburg Publishing House, 1978.

Jensen, I. L. *Jensen's Survey of the Old Testament.* Chicago, IL: Moody Press, 1978.

Kempis, T. *The Imitation of Christ.* London: Oxford University Press, 1920.

Kenyon, E. W. *The Blood Covenant, 28th ed.* Lynnwood, WA: Kenyon's Gospel Publishing Society, 1969.

KJV-Amplified Holy Bible: Parallel Bible. Grand Rapids, MI: Zondervan Publishing House, 1995.

Leonard, E. G., Reid, J. M., trans. and ed. Rowley, H. H. *A History of Protestantism: The Reformation,. Vol. 1.* Indianapolis, IN: Bobbs-Merill, 1968.

Loewen, Harry and Nolt, Steven. *Through Fire & Water: An Overview of Mennonite History.* Scottsdale, PA: Herald Press, 1996.

Lohse, M. *Martin Luther: An Introduction to His Life and Work.* Philadelphia, PA: Fortress Press, 1986.

Luther, M. *Ninety-Five Theses: Address to the German Nobility Concerning Christian Liberty.* New York: Collier, 1965.

Manns, P. *Martin Luther: An Illustrated Biography.* New York: Crossroad, 1982.

Mjorud, H. *What's Baptism All About?* Carol Stream, IL: Creation House, 1978.

Murray, A. *The Power of the Blood of Jesus.* Springdale, PA: Whitaker House, 1993.

Norris, R. A., Jr. *The Christological Controversy.* Philadelphia, PA: Fortress Press, 1980.

Oberman, H. *Luther: A Man Between God and the Devil.* New Haven, CT: Yale University Press, 1989.

O'Donnell, J. J. *Augustine.* Boston, MA: Twayne Publishers, 1985.

Office of the Presbyterian General Assembly. *The Work of the Holy Spirit.* Philadelphia, PA: United Presbyterian Church in the United States of America, 1978.

O'Neill, J. *Martin Luther.* New York: Cambridge University Press, 1975.

Oyer, J. S. and Kreider, R. S. *Mirror of the Martyrs.* Intercourse, PA: Good Books, 1990.

Prince, D. *Appointment in Jerusalem.* Grand Rapids, MI: Chosen Books, 1975.

Reimer, M. L., ed. *Christians Courageous.* Waterloo, Ontario: Mennonite Publishing Service, 1988.

Richardson, D. *Eternity in Their Hearts.* Ventura, CA: Regal Books, 1981.

Rost, S., ed. *Martin Luther: The Best From All His Works.* Nashville, TN: Thomas Nelson, 1989.

Sachar, Leon, Ph.D. *A History of the Jew, 5th ed.* New York: Alfred A. Knopf, 1967.

Simon, E. *Luther Alive: Martin Luther and the Making of the Reformation.* Garden City, NY: Doubleday, 1968.

Schmeman, Alexander. *The Historical Road of Eastern Orthodoxy.*

Smith, C. H. *Story of the Mennonites.* Newton, KS: Mennonite Publication Office, 1950.

Spitz, L. W. *The Protestant Reformation.* Englewood Cliffs, NJ: Prentice-Hall, 1966.

Strong, J. *The Strong's Exhaustive Concordance of the Bible.* Nashville, TN: Thomas Nelson Publishers, 1996.

Tenney, M. C. *New Testament Times.* Grand Rapids, MN: Wm B. Erdmans Publishing Company, 1978.

Todd, J. M. *Luther.* New York: Crossroad, 1982.

Trumbull, H. C. *The Blood Covenant: A Primitive Rite and Its Bearing on Scripture.* Kirkwood, MO: Impact Books, 1975.

Van Braght, T. J. *Martyrs Mirror.* Scottsdale, PA: Herald Press, 1950.

The Waldenses. Angwin, CA: LLT Productions.

White, Ellen G. *The Great Controversy.* Mt. View, CA: Pacific Press Publ. Assn., 1956.

Whyte, Rev. H. A. M. *The Power of the Blood.* Springdale, PA: Whitaker House, 1973.

"Worshipping Like Pagans?" *Christian History,* Issue 37.

Yandian, B. *Galatians: The Spirit-Controlled Life.* Tulsa, OK: Pillar Book & Publishing Company, 1993.